AF879764

ISBN: Paperback 978-1-64873-161-7
ISNB: EBOOK 978-1-64873-162-4

Printed in the United States of America
Published by:
Writer's Publishing House
Prescott, Az 86301

Cover and Interior Design by Creative Artistic Excellence Marketing
Project Management and Book Launch by Creative Artistic Excellence Marketing https://lizzymcnett.com

HUDCO Scam Series

Book Two

Government HUDCO Andrews Ganj Scam

By Alborz Azar
alborzazar.net

Table of Contents

Acknowledgment

I acknowledge my sincere thanks to my Lawyer friends at Delhi for providing voluminous documents regarding Andrews Ganj Land at Delhi. The efforts put in by my several Advocates friends even in the Covid period are being appreciated by me. Many of my other friends in Delhi also helped me to get the documents from the Ministry of Urban Development and HUDCO, which I sincerely acknowledge their efforts made to make me write the truth about Andrews Ganj

Introduction

In the Andrews Ganj Scam, the heterogeneous magnitude of the scandals has always raised questions about the plausible, transparent, and responsive Indian Government policies in different eras. So many of these scams have ripped off the entire economy of India over the years.

The Bofors scandal of 1980 & the 90s for about Rs. 150 crores (US Dollar 85.71 million) are known as the hallmark of Indian corruption. The Bofors scam was a major corruption scandal in India in the 1980s; when the then PM Rajiv Gandhi and several others, including a powerful NRI family named the Hinduja, alleged as accused of receiving kickbacks from Bofors AB for winning a bid to supply India's 155 mm field howitzer. Most of all, the Bofors scam had a strong emotional appeal because it was a scam related to the defense services and India's security interests.

The Hawala case to the tune of the US Dollar 18 million bribery scandal in 1990-1991 for about Rs. 100 crores (US Dollar 43.97 million) which came in the open in 1996, involved payments allegedly received by the country's leading politicians through hawala brokers. Thus, for the first time in Indian politics, it gave a feeling of open loot all around the public, involving all the major political players being accused of having accepted bribes and also alleged connections about payments being channeled to Hizbul Mujahideen militants in Kashmir.

The question is how HUDCO has received the buy product "HUDCO Place" at Andrews Ganj constructing illegal properties, violating all the laws of the country in the shadow of the Congress Government resulting in a third time Scam of the Andrews Ganj land. Who else will be scammed by HUDCO? The biggest scam of Andrews Ganj goes undisclosed to date. It still awaits the mayhem in the world of the public sector. In the next books, we will see how skillfully HUDCO along with the Ministry of Urban Affairs dupes which corporate.

What is disappointing to see is the pattern of the Government, Bureaucrats, Public Sectors duping the public at large by building unauthorized constructions and getting away under the name of the legal game. Government fraud in the public sectors goes scot-free under the system created in the country.

While notorious builders will go to jail, they do not catch the games by officers of the public sector in power. If a private builder builds an unauthorized construction, they demolish the same and the sufferer would be allotted those buildings. The builders resultantly would be liable to go behind bars. But in India it is not wrong if a public sector company holds the funds collected for the unauthorized constructions and the installments paid by the buyers, it has not held them to be liable to refund and neither are they liable for punishment under the criminal law as they are the Government companies.

Chapter: One

Andrews Ganj Land Scam from 1950 to 1985

As my series on India land scams continues, in the second book I want to bring light onto the Bofors scandal of 1980 and 1990s. In the previous book, I covered the HUCO's land scam enveloping the precious Andrews Ganj Land. Various Ministries, Institutions, Private Builders, Hoteliers, and Big Business Houses eyed the property in India. At the latter part of the situation, the land has been entrusted to officers of HUDCO at the behest of the Congress Government, who completely mismanaged all construction. In their haste, they built guesthouse blocks with car parks in the basement without approvals of Municipal Corporation of Delhi, the Fire department, and the Delhi Urban Art Commission.

The story of the Andrews Ganj began before establishing the separation of Bharat as India and Pakistan in 1947, after the English granted independence. In 1950, Congress leased out the precious land at Aliganj, as named earlier to the Pinjrapole Society. The agreement stated in the garb was for housing cows and buffaloes. But otherwise used by Pinjrapole Society for sub-leasing the property to various persons. The society neglected to pay lease fees of Rs. 25,000/- (US Dollar 2021) per annum, but continued to keep the land under its possession till 1985 when finally, the Supreme Court came to the rescue of Andrews Ganj land and had directed to vacate the land by 30th May 1985.

In 1985, Congress allotted part of the Andrews Ganj land to nine societies belonging to the Members of Parliament and the Officers of the Ministry of Urban Development. Finally, the Supreme Court again came to the rescue of Andrews Ganj land on 5th April 1989 and got the land vacated from these societies by refunding the amounts paid with 12 percent interest.

Thereafter, possession of the land was given to HUDCO in 1989. The company began to construct the buildings with no sanction of building plans. In total, this was the third scam of Andrew Ganj's land, as the present value of the land is Rs. 5000/- Crores (US Dollar 657.89 million) allotted to HUDCO @ Re. 1/- per acre for 32 years' lease. Book 1 of Andrew's Ganj Land Scam ends in 1989 from the partition and independence of India. The Government HUDCO Andrews Ganj Scam continues from January 1990, till 31st March 1994.

In the meantime, the additional secretary Mr. R.K. Takkar who was handling Andrews Ganj land until December 1989 was transferred in the first week of January 1990. The

Government with Mr. V.P. Singh took over as Prime Minister of India on 2nd December 1989. Mr. Murasoli Maran, the Minister of Urban Development changed on 6th December 1989, who brought in his officers in the Ministry. The new additional secretary handling Andrews Ganj land was Mr. P.P. Srivastava.

HOUSING & URBAN DEVELOPMENT CORPORATION LTD. (HUDCO)

HUDCO was incorporated as 'The Housing and Urban Development Finance Corporation Private Limited' on 25th April 1970. They became a private limited company under the Companies Act of 1956, and a certificate of incorporation by the Registrar of Companies. Subsequently, the name of the company changed to 'Housing and Urban Development Corporation Limited' on July 9, 1974. The Registrar of Companies Delhi & Haryana issued a fresh certificate of incorporation. The Company is a public sector undertaking fully owned by the Ministry of Urban Development.

In 1996, the Department of Company Affairs was notified as a public financial institution under Section 4A of the Companies Act 1956 the company, Ministry of Finance,

Government of India. HUDCO began retail financing by lending to the private borrower companies @ 14 to 18 percent compounded monthly. The amounts received from MS Shoes were kept fraudulently from the year 1994-1995 to date. Plus, they lent the same amounts to borrowers.

My dear readers, the series of events is a protruding unusual situation; a transaction resulting in the scam by the Government and HUDCO in handing over possession of the land with no documentation. The most precious 71-acres at Andrews Ganj given to HUDCO, which is a company under the Companies Act, 1956, which is required to follow laws applicable as per the company.

Chapter: Two

Urgency of Afro Asian Games, 1992

It has been revealed to me from the documents collected, in pursuance to HUDCO's intimation of the meeting on 15th January 1990. The meeting was held in the presence of officers of the Ministry and concerned officials of HUDCO, ignoring the plans submitted by the Central Public Works Department, Municipal Corporation of Delhi, and the Delhi Urban Art Commission for consideration. The Ministry wanted HUDCO to develop Andrews Ganj land due to which HUDCO was required to submit the building plans.

In the absence of any formal allotment, the favor was granted to HUDCO of Andrews Ganj land. Thereby, HUDCO could not have submitted any building plans as it had no official authority to deal with Andrews Ganj land.

The result of HUDCO's development and construction at Andrews Ganj would be revealed in Book Three "HUDCO Place Andrews Ganj Land Scam" and "Book Four- Andrews Ganj Land Scam Continuing" of the HUDCO Scam Series. The advice of the Central Public Works Department, Senior Architect, neglected rather deliberately to avoid the result from the HUDCO Scam on Andrews Ganj Land at Delhi.

The Liaison Officer of Central Public Works Department, Mr. G.S. Minocha, informed on 2nd January 1990 to Mr. M.B. Sexena, Senior Architect, Central Public Works Department regarding General Pool Housing at Pinjrapole (Andrews Ganj) that the requirements of the Community Center at Pinjrapole are fixed based entirely on the local needs of the area in the near vicinity, and as per the Zonal text / Zonal planning by Delhi Development Authority. It is considered basically for the F-3 zone, and not at city-level, as it is only planned as a Zonal Community Center. The only exact requirements proposed and provided in the compressive/ integrated scheme in drawing No. TP-3265/R are to be followed strictly.

- Total Ground Coverage = 15,840 M2 OR (22.23%)
- Total Floor Area = 71,802 M2 OR (100.8) excess to be adjusted.
- Area of Plot= 17.6 ACRES OR 71,227.2 M2.
- Permissible Ground = 25% OR 17,806.8 M2
- Coverage Permissible Far =100 OR 71,227.2 M2

On 8th January 1990 Chairman-cum-Managing Director of HUDCO and Mr. S.K. Sharma requested all concerned to a meeting on 15th January 1990 at 4.00 pm in HUDCO's office. Including:

- Mr. PP Srivastava,
- Additional Secretary, Ministry of Urban Development
- Mr. K Dharmarajan, Jt. Secretary (Lands),
- Ministry of Urban Development,
- Mr. MK Rishi, Chief Architect,
- Central Public Works Department
- Mr. SC Gupta, Director (Planning), Delhi Development Authority.
- Mr. S Auluck, Sr. Architect,
- Delhi Development Authority.
- Mr. Arjun Dev, Chief Architect,
- Municipal Corporation of Delhi,
- Mr. DD Mathur, Town Planner,
- Municipal Corporation of Delhi, Mr. Ravindra Bhan,
- Architect. Mr. Jasbir Sawhney, Consultant Regarding Urban Design of Community Center

Further, informing all officers that after incorporating the modifications suggested in the meeting, the urban design will be finalized and submitted with the model to the ministry after a week for submission to the Municipal Corporation of Delhi /Delhi Urban Art Commission.

Concurrently, Delhi Development Authority will be requested to confirm the planning regulations to avoid delay in the scrutiny by the local authorities.

On the other hand, Mr. M.B. Saxena Senior Architect, Central Public Works Department, represented on 11th January 1990 to Mr. P.P. Srivastava, Additional Secretary Regarding General Pool Housing at Pinjrapole Andrews Ganj, New Delhi. (Comprehensive scheme along with Community Center) enclosing a copy of the revised drg. No. IP-3265/R showing also residential areas. The detailed planning for the Community Center on a plot area of 17.6 acres.

Further, confirming the requirements of the Community Center are based on a master plan and zonal plan prepared by the Delhi Development Authority. The total scheme satisfied the local body's norms and waited for approval from Delhi Urban Art Commission as well. It may be mentioned this scheme showing the residential portion submitted to Delhi Municipal Corporation on 10.12.1989 for their necessary approval and submission to Delhi Urban Art Commission. It shall also be appropriate to mention here that if it is desired to change the scheme at this stage, it is likely to delay the sports authority of India's requirements/rooms, which are a part of this comprehensive scheme.

The Central Public Works Department in its honesty continued to follow the approval layout plans submitted to Municipal Corporation of Delhi and Delhi Urban Art Commission with the Town Planner, Municipal Corporation of Delhi regarding General Pool Accommodation Housing for Sports Authority of India Pinjrapole New Delhi on 19th January 1990. The right of way existing and proposed roads was already mentioned on the submitted drawing. In the detailed section of proposed roads, it also shows the 4 storied blocks are at 2 meters from feeder 4.5 meters wished roads. In the case of multistoried blocks, the feeder 6 meters wide road runs around touching the building blocks (Ground floor being completely on stilts) as per fire regulations.

The zonal development plan has been followed completely. Approval of the Delhi Urban Art Commission can only be obtained when, as per the latest guidelines from Delhi Urban Art Commission, it is forwarded to them by the office. The necessary proforma has been duly filed and submitted in your office on 16.12.1989 only. You are requested to please forward the same to Delhi Urban Art

Commission so that their approval can be obtained for your further necessary action.

Simultaneously, the Central Public Works Department's Senior Architect, Mr. M.B. Saxena, on 19th January 1990 honestly requested to the Additional Secretary, Ministry of Urban Development regarding General Pool Accommodation Housing at Pinjrapole, Andrews Ganj, in continuation to the meeting held on 15th January 1990 at HUDCO's office, explaining that this office wishes to place before you the following information for your kind consideration and necessary instructions.

After much deliberation on various alternatives by Central Public Works Department for General Pool Housing at Pinjrapole site, the Ministry of Urban Development vide the minutes of the meeting held on 18th August 1989 at 4 pm under the chairmanship of Mr. R.K. Takkar, Additional Secretary approved the above-referred housing scheme and instructed the department to prepare and submit the final proposal of housing to be submitted to Delhi Urban Art Commission for their necessary approval. In the same meeting, it was also decided that HUDCO would do the work of development of the Community Center on the ear-marked site of 17.6 acres instead of 7 acres.

It was decided in the meeting held on 7th November 1989 with the Secretary, Ministry of Urban Development, the Central Public Works Department would obtain approval from Delhi Urban Art Commission for General Pool Housing and Housing for Afro Asian Games being the Nation's Commitment. As the Delhi Urban Art Commission requires the design, including the Community Center, HUDCO, as well as the Central Public Works Department, would prepare a comprehensive development plan. However, in this process, the request was made to push the Sports Authority housing faster, so the staff would have a living quarter for the upcoming Afro Asian Games.

It shall be proper to mention the proposal of land use distribution as suggested by the HUDCO Architect was mainly favorable to the planning of the Community Center, however, due to this distribution, the housing was pushed to a very tight place sandwiching the scheme between fly-over on the east, type I & II accommodation just abutting on north and south i.e., Andrews Ganj & Sadiq Nagar. Basically, this housing shall have no identity of its own, nor have any frontage/elevation on the main road.

As an author of this book to reveal the truth, I had to go through the voluminous documents and the correspondences which showed the new Additional Secretary knew little about the developments of Andrews Ganj land and was only briefed by the Joint Secretary, Mr. Dharmarajan, as he had been part of the previous meetings and decisions before the previous Additional Secretary, Mr. R.K. Takkar. Central Public Works Department's Senior Architect, Mr. M.B. Saxena had honestly advised the Ministry but seems HUDCO was on the winning side, as HUDCO's Chairman-cum-Managing Director and its officers kept proximity to all the officers and the Minister of Urban Development to get the Andrews Ganj land at any cost.

Dear readers, isn't it a scam that HUDCO was a company whose main object was to lend money, and who had no experience in constructions or handling a big chunk of land at Andrews Ganj, but the Government bi passed Central Public Works Department and Delhi Development Authority, who had the authority to handle such land and construction projects?

Is it that the Government can do anything that they feel like every 5 years the ruling party's Government could be changed?

Chapter: Three

HUDCO Submitted Benefit Analysis

HUDCO continued to plan the construction at Andrews Ganj as per the new master plan for Delhi, 2001, and neglected the restrictions of the zonal development plan F-3 Zone, and submitted for approval to the Ministry by manipulating with the planning department of the Delhi Development Authority. The Director Mr. S.C. Gupta put up the report to Joint Director Mr. Prakash Narayan and Deputy Director (Master Planning) Mr. Surendra Shrivastava for approval as per the report submitted on 22nd January 1990 by the Chairman of HUDCO.

It was strongly informed that, as per the proposal submitted, there is a provision for 5-star hotels, restaurants, and shops in the Community Center. The general experience of a 5-star hotel in Delhi shows that most of the hotels were facing a parking shortage during marriages and conferences. Thus, it may be better if some additional parking space is also identified and provided in the complex.

Central Public Works Department continued to pursue on 23rd January 1990 with Delhi Urban Art Commission for conceptual approval of General Pool Housing and Housing for Sports Authority of India at Pinjrapole New Delhi (including Community Center) at Pinjrapole on a 71.2 Acres, further submitting plan T-3265/R. Central Public Works Department further confirmed to Delhi Urban Art Commission that the scheme has been submitted to the Municipal Corporation of Delhi on 16th December 1989, but as there is a National Commitment to construct and make quarters for Sports Authority of India before the Afro-Asian Games, i.e. by October 1991, the additional Secretary, Ministry of Urban Development, has instructed this office for forwarding the Scheme with Model and Repot, etc., to Delhi Urban Art Commission immediately.

HUDCO's appointed Architect, Mr. Jasbir Sawhney & Associates, informed on 25th January 1990 to Mr. S.K. Sharma, Chairman-cum-Managing Director HUDCO regarding Urban Design for Community Center enclosing the Site Analysis report identifying the traffic system and land use. The land use identifies the location of the Community Center, Zonal Green, and Housing. These reports recommend the Zonal Green be kept as a consolidated buffer space between the Community Center and the Housing. A plan is showing the land use, and it is requested that we may ask the Delhi Development Authority to give their approval since this is urban design development for the zonal plan prepared by the Delhi Development Authority.

HUDCO's Chairman-cum-Managing Director, Mr. S.K. Sharma, on 30th January 1990, clarified to Mr. Shrivastav, Additional Secretary, Ministry of Urban Development, recalling the informal discussion with Delhi Urban Art Commission regarding Urban Design of Andrews Ganj Institutional Area and Housing, the members had appreciated the design of the Community Center. Where housing is concerned, Chief Architect, Central Public Works Department on 19th January 1990, expressed certain difficulties planning 1454 units in the 35 acres available for housing. We have attempted a layout in which 1454 housing units in an attractive environment eliminate the heavy expenses associated with multistoried buildings.

HUDCO proposed 350 housing units are to be constructed for the Afro Asian Games on a priority basis. One solution could be that HUDCO can construct these houses, as per we can adjust its designs and the expenditure against the cost of land of the Community Center. We can construct the dining hall complex for Afro Asian Games, according to Laurie Baker's system.

Andrew Ganj Community Center Urban Design Cost-Benefit Analysis (Provisional)

- Land area 17 acres of 71,000 sq. meter FAR 100
- Buildable is 71,000 sq. meter
- Cost of developed land @ Rs. 10,800 per sq. meter Rs. 76 crores (US Dollar 617) Dollar 43.42 million)
- Less cost of site development @ Rs. 600 per sq. Rs 4 cores (US Dollar 34.28) Dollar 2.28 million)
- Development of 18 acres (10 ha) Rs. 4 crores (US Dollar 2.28 million)
- Zonal green @ Rs 400 per sq cost of undeveloped land payable by Rs. 68 crores (US Dollar 38.85 million)
- HUDCO to ministry
- Construction costs Rs 5000 per sq. Rs. 35 crores (US Dollar 20 million)
- Cost of central parking Rs. 8 crores (US Dollar 4.57 million) Total outflow of HUDCO (No 4+7+8) Rs. 119 crores (US Dollar 68 million)
- Institutional space sold at no profit, no loss 20% of total built space 14,200 sq. meter.

- Area saleable at market price 56,800 sq. meter
- Price recovered for institutional space Rs. 15,000 per sq. meter Rs. 21 crores (US Dollar 857.14) Dollar 12 million)
- Price recovered for balance area at an average market price of Rs. 114 crores (US Dollar 65.14 million) 20,000 per sq
- Total inflow of HUDCO Rs 135 crores (US Dollar 77.14 million)
- Net surplus for HUDCO Rs. 16 crores (US Dollar 9.14 million)

To enable us to invest in the project, the arrangement between the Ministry and HUDCO regarding the land for the Community Center will also have to be finalized. They had submitted a preliminary cost-benefit analysis prepared. It will be observed the project is viable, and HUDCO can make a small surplus after defraying Rs. 68 crores (US Dollar 38.75 million) to the Ministry against the cost of land.

In the meantime, Mahanagar Telephone Nigam Ltd. Requested for 1-1/2 acres of land at Andrews Ganj for a telephone exchange, which was recommended on 14th

February 1990 to Chairman-cum-Managing Director, HUDCO by Mr. Rakesh Mehta Director (Land), Ministry of Urban Development to incorporate in the urban design being prepared by HUDCO.

As an author, it appears HUDCO somehow wanted to grab the precious Andrews Ganj land.

Wasn't it a trick to propose to realize extra monies from the private parties by HUDCO on behalf of the Government planning the construction at Andrews Ganj as per the new master plan for Delhi, 2001, and neglected the restrictions of the zonal development plan F-3 Zone?

Chapter: Four

Constructions Started by HUDCO Without Approvals of Building Plans from Local Bodies

As the author, which would also make the readers believe Ministry unofficially permitted HUDCO to go on with constructions without the approval of Delhi Urban Art Commission, Municipal Corporation of Delhi, Town Planner, Fire Department, Delhi Development Authority, Land & Development Office, etc., considering that nobody will stop the constructions as they are being carried out for and by the Government of India.

In the meantime, in the second week of February 1990, the honest man, Mr. M.B. Saxena, who was Chief Architect of Central Public Works Department, was appointed Secretary of Delhi Urban Art Commission, who was fully aware of Andrews Ganj land developments replacing Mr. J.J. S. Majithia.

HUDCO's Architect, Mr. Jasbir Sawhney & Associates, submitted on 15th February 1990 the layout plan drawing for conceptual urban design for 71 acres at Andrews Ganj to Mr. J.J.S. Majithia, Secretary, Delhi Urban Art Commission, as he was unaware that Mr. M.B. Saxena had become the Secretary of Delhi Urban Art Commission.

- Government Pool Housing - 35.6 acres
- Zonal Parking - 18.00 acres

- Community Center - 17.6 acres

The drawings were placed in the 595th meeting of The Delhi Urban Art Commission Head On February 15, 1990, there were various members of Delhi Urban Art Commission present - Mr. Abid Hussain-Chairman, Mr. P. P Shrivastava-Member, Mr. Ravindra Bhan - Member, Mr. Sharat Das–Member, Mr. M. B Saxena–Secretary, Mr. J.J. S Majithia–Urban Designer, Mr. R. Vaidya - Architect Planner, Mr. D. D Madan - Administrative Officer and Mr. Vinod Kumar- Dy. Architect and Advisers - Mr. Jasbir Sachdev, Mr. Raj Rewal, Mr. S. C Gupta

The proposal submitted by the consultant, Mr. Jasbir Sawhney, was considered at Item-10 as an Additional Item being proposed development at Pinjrapole at the preliminary conceptual stage for an informal discussion. At the behest of Mr. P.P. Srivastava, the members of the Commission applied their mind to the two alternative layouts (one prepared by the Central Public Works Department and the other by HUDCO's consultant Mr. Jasbir Sawhney) for informal advice. There were various revisions advised informally by the members of the Delhi Urban Art Commission, observing that after incorporating the suggested revisions, the commission would consider after receiving through the Municipal Corporation of Delhi the local body.

The Urban Design Scheme was prepared by HUDCO and presented to the Ministry of Urban Development on 21st February 1990, in which the officers present were, Mr. KC Sivaramakrishnan, Secretary (UD), Mr. P.P. Shrivastav, Additional Secretary, Ministry of Urban Development, Mr. B. Bhattacharya, Joint Secretary (Finance) Ministry of Urban Development, Mr. P.S.A. Sundaram, Joint Secretary (H), Ministry of Urban Development, Mr. S.K. Sharma, Chairman-cum-Managing Director, HUDCO, Mr. Jasbir Sawhney, Architect Consultant, HUDCO.
Chairman-cum-Managing Director, HUDCO explained the urban design scheme prepared by HUDCO, as presented before Delhi Urban Art Commission to the Secretary, Ministry of Urban Development, the design had provided a central green spine, which got linked with the Community Center through the zonal green. In this manner, high environmental quality in low rise but high-density development had been achieved.

Mr. P. P Shrivastava, Additional Secretary, Ministry of Urban Development, explained that a total of 350 houses with common facilities like dining, office, shops, etc. had to be provided for the Afro Asian Games, whereas the Central Public Works Department was constructing on 256. An additional 100 houses and common facilities also need to be constructed on a priority basis.

HUDCO has submitted a proposal that, in place of the cost of the land of the Community Center, HUDCO can build and provide housing to the Ministry. Agreeing that this concept appeared attractive from a commercial standpoint. Joint Secretary (Finance), who is appointed in the Ministry by the Ministry of Finance to protect the interest of the Government, pointed out that this posed certain procedural difficulties in Government transactions and will have to be sorted out in consultation with the Finance Ministry. Chairman-cum-Managing Director, HUDCO informed that while normally the development of district centers and Community Centers in Delhi is done by Delhi Development Authority, in a meeting by the Additional Secretary, Ministry of Urban Development on 26th July 1989, in which Delhi Development Authority and HUDCO representatives were present, it was agreed the Community

Center in Andrews Ganj be entrusted to HUDCO. However, within a few months, HUDCO has furnished an urban design for Andrews Gang in which they have incorporated various innovative concepts.

He added it appeared from the discussions that the flats have to be made available for the Afro Asian Games in November 1991. The time available is inadequate, and unless immediate steps are taken for finalizing the detailed designs and undertaking the construction, it will be impossible to complete the facilities in time. Chairman-cum-Managing Director, HUDCO stressed that possession of land earmarked for Community Center zonal green and housing, excluding the portion in which Central Public Works Department would be constructing 256 houses, was handed over to HUDCO with the stipulation that HUDCO should go ahead with preparation Community Center and immediate construction of houses and common facilities for the Afro Asian Games, subject to finalization of the terms and conditions as between the Ministry and HUDCO in due course.

It was agreed by the then Secretary of the Ministry of Urban Development that in the meantime, HUDCO should incur expenditure on the Government Pool housing subject to adjustment later. HUDCO consultant will also interact and coordinate with the Chief Architect, Central Public Works Department, to finalize the layout and external development of the 256 houses being constructed by the Central Public Works Department following the urban design. It was agreed to in principle because of the urgency of development so that 350 residential units (including 256 by the Central Public Works Department) and other ancillary structures had to be completed well in time for being put to use in Afro-Asian Games in 1991.

Joint Secretary (Finance) pointed out that although the unofficial possession of the land has been given to HUDCO, who has started the construction. But officially there were certain difficulties in immediately handing over possession on paper since the nine cooperative societies to whom plots were earlier allotted out of this land had to be refunded the money paid by them with an interest in terms of the Supreme Court judgment before the Government can officially on paper take over possession of the land.

The Additional Secretary, Ministry of Urban Development, informed the Ministry was taking appropriate action, and this problem was likely to be solved in a fortnight. In the meantime, they decided HUDCO may go ahead with detailed engineering designs, tendering, etc., and the constructions started to be continued by HUDCO without the approval of layout plans or other plans.

HUDCO also informed the present officers that in their last board meeting, the developments regarding the urban design of Community Center and housing in Andrews Ganj, and the Board had approved undertaking further work in anticipation of Government approval. The Officers of the Ministry decided along with the Secretary of the Ministry of Urban Development that the official approval and official hand over of possession of the land excluding the land which will be used by the Central Public Works Department for construction of 256 houses pending finalization of lease deed and other conditions will be given to HUDCO. The Ministry will give in writing to go ahead with the construction of 100 houses, dining, and other common facilities required for the Afro Asian Games 1991, in addition to 256 houses being constructed by the Central Public Works Department pending finalization of financial arrangements.

HUDCO also held discussions with the Secretary (Sports) in this regard. He said that if the 500 guesthouse rooms in the Community Center could also be constructed and made available for the Afro Asian Games 1991, along with the development of the zonal green, it would create an attractive environment and be extremely useful for the games. HUDCO informed the Secretary that considerable design and development work was involved in the Guesthouses, and as such it could give no such assurance. However, every effort would be made to ascertain if we could make whole or part of these Guesthouses available.

As author HUDCO and the Ministry of Urban Development were well aware that the approval from the Municipal Corporation of Delhi and Delhi Urban Art Commission and the Fire Department was mandatory before the start of construction at Andrews Ganj. The comments of HUDCO to the Ministry of Urban Development clearly state "if the project is to be completed within time, but continued, the Ministry will construct the buildings with no approvals and sanctions."

Wasn't it a confidence game by the Government and HUDCO jointly by starting constructions at Andrews Ganj without the sanction of building plans with the proposal to sell without such approvals?

Chapter: Five

Central Public Works Department Versus HUDCO

It reveals to me from the documents that the Central Public Works Department was still keen to go on with the entire project on Andrews Ganj land, and had already gone ahead in submissions of the urban design of the 71 acres as the owner of the land, and had undertaken there is no construction undertaken on the land which will be started only after approval of the plans by the competent authority. However, HUDCO continued its own game to own Andrews Ganj's land somehow or the other.

Mr. M.B. Saxena, Secretary, Delhi Urban Art Commission and Chief Architect, Central Public Works Department, informed on 9th March 1990 to Mr. P.P. Srivastava, Member, Delhi Urban Art Commission and Additional Secretary of the Ministry of Urban Development regarding the proposed development at Pinjrapole at the preliminary conceptual stage for informal discussion held on 15th February 1990 meeting of Delhi Urban Art Commission, conveying the observations made by Delhi Urban Art Commission in the meeting. It was further stated these observations are not being conveyed to anyone else, since we informally discussed the matter at the preliminary conceptual stage.

On perusal by Central Public Works Department on the application submitted before Municipal Corporation of Delhi, the Municipal Corporation of Delhi Officer Mr. P.D. Singhal, Architect, informed the Secretary Delhi Urban Art Commission on 15th March 1990 regarding Layout Plan for General Pool Housing for Sports Authority of India at Pinjrapole, New Delhi informing that Central Public Works Department has submitted a proposal for construction of Type IV, V & VI quarters varying from 4 to 12 storied and hostels also 8 to 12 storied for General Pool Housing for sports authority of India on a total plot area of 71.20 acres i.e. site for proposed Community Center (Not part of the present proposal) and zonal green as per zonal plan, balance is being–for residential and commonly facility sites. Two sites for Primary School, 5 sites for Nursery Schools Kinder ESS, Convenient Shopping, Dining Hall, etc.

Municipal Corporation of Delhi-to-Delhi Urban Art Commission to consider the scheme at the conceptual stage, with observations made, forwarded two sets of layout plans. We have also advised the Architect of the Central Public Works Department to submit necessary drawings, models, photographs, etc. directly to the Commission and get the conceptual approval of the scheme.

Proforma of Planning Permission Forwarded to Delhi Urban Art Commission by Municipal Corporation of Delhi:

1.1	**Title**	General Pool Housing & Housing for Sports Authority of India at Pinjrapole, New Delhi
1.2	**Location**	Pinjrapole between Andrews Gang & Sadiq Nagar, New Delhi
1.3	**Owner**	Executive Engineer, MBRH Project Central Public Works Department, Ministry of Urban Development
1.4	**Promoter**	Ministry of Urban Development
1.5	**Architect** **(Also give address and telephone no.)**	Mr. S.N. Segal, Architect (H&TP) I Room No. 307A, Central Public Works Department, Nirman Bhawan, New Delhi. Phone–3019681
2.4	**Council of Architecture: Regn. No. of Architect**	CA/79/4906

2.5	**Structural Consultant**	Central Public Works Department
2.6	**Landscape Consultant**	Central Public Works Department
3.1	**Net Plot area of overall complex** **Net Plot area under Resi. Scheme.**	71.20 acres 35.60 acres
3.2	**Land use:** **Master Plan** **Zonal Development Plan** **Approved Layout Plan**	Residential As per Zonal Plan F.3 Zone, Zonal Green of residential with two primary school sites Nil -
3.3	**Regulations** **Envelop control/ setback** **Ground Coverage (%)** **FAR** **Height**	Front 40- 'O', Sides/Rear Min.- 5.0 Mt Max-12.0 Mt 25% 175 Restriction up to 80 Car, Scooter

	Parking norms **Green Area and Ply-field** **Density (Gross)** **Community Facilities**	Zonal Green + 50% Res. Plot. 60 dirs. per acre Convenient Shopping ESS–2 nos. Pining Hall, Primary School
4.1	**Existing Development** **No. of Building blocks and nomenclature** **Ground Coverage** **FAR** **Height**	Nil Nil Nil Nil
4.2	**Proposal** **Ground Coverage** **FAR** **Heights**	22.82 say 23% 146.48 Maximum height 39.0 Mt. including water tank
4.3	**Total (existing proposed)** **Ground Coverage**	22.82 say 23% 146.48

FAR	As per Zonal Plan
Green Areas	Gross density -40.8 per acre
Density	For 4st building100% surface parking
Parking Provision	For M.S. building 100% basement parking

Delhi Development Authority in March 1990 made observations in charge of the Master Plan, knowing that the present land use as per Master Plan, 2001, Andrews Ganj land can be used for Convention Center and Institutions for Social and Cultural purposes. The residential construction could only be carried out as per Master Plan, 1962, and then the Community Center could only be developed as given in Master Plan, 1962.

On HUDCO's insistence, on 16th March 1990, Mr. Surendra Srivastava, Dy. Director (Master Plan) submitted the critical appraisal of the report forwarded by HUDCO regarding the convention center at Siri Fort. It may be better if we could discuss this case in the Delhi Development Authority for some decisions which have to be taken on the subject in terms of land use. Residential as per Master Plan for Delhi-62 or Social & Cultural as per draft PDP-2001, size of Convention Center, Hotels, etc. & also the traffic circulation.

Isn’t it that HUDCO and Government developed and constructed at Andrews Ganj as per Master Plan, 2001 to make a quick profit, and proposed a fraudulent scheme knowingly that the hotel and the Guesthouses could not be allowed at Andrews Ganj as per Master Plan 1962?

Chapter: Six

Authorization by Ministry of Urban Development to HUDCO To Continue to Construct

Any prudent person could understand they submitted the layout plans at the conceptual stage, Municipal Corporation of Delhi or Delhi Urban Art Commission, without following the Zonal Development Plan and the Master Plan, 2001 could not consider. But HUDCO continued to submit the unauthorized plan of the layout which was not as per Master Plan, 2001 and kept pressurizing the Municipal Corporation of Delhi and Delhi Urban Art Commission through the Ministry of Urban Development for approval of a layout plan which could not be approved without the change of land use of Andrews Ganj land.

The readers would realize HUDCO was in dispute with the Central Public Works Department, as HUDCO was in the greed of the entire land. Mr. S.K. Sharma Chairman-cum-Managing Director HUDCO communicated on 9th April 1990 to Mr. Srivastava, Additional Secretary (Urban Development) Central Public Works Department that while developing the urban design of the 71 acres of land near Andrews Ganj, we proposed a layout of 256 flats as per Central Public Works Department layout. In a meeting convened by you, the Central Public Works Department did not accept our layout and insisted the layout should strictly conform to their configuration. We have accordingly done another exercise, a note along with a drawing delineating 10 acres for Central Public Works Department (9 acres for housing and 1 acre for the proposed flyover on Tito Marg alongside.

As the author goes through, the documents show that playing a clever game. HUDCO's Chairman-cum-Managing Director indirectly attempting to maneuver explained in the note that our earlier proposal was more economical both inland and construction. Due to low density in the Central Public Works Department layout, 9 acres instead of 7 acres are queried for accommodating 256 units. This loss of 2 acres will result in a reduction of 100 units in the layout. The one-acre reduction of another 50 units. Thus, against the 1450 units provided earlier, there will now be 1300 units in the layout.

Our consultants had proposed another design of the flyover on Tito Marg, which provides better circulation and will not need one-acre land from the housing area. Director Planning, Delhi Development Authority supported our proposal, but the Delhi Administration, Municipal Corporation of Delhi has not accepted it. You may like to convene a meeting to review the matter. If they accept our proposal, the Central Public Works Department will get another acre in which they can later build some units.

HUDCO also sent a copy of this letter to the Chief Architect, Central Public Works Department, for further necessary action.

Thereafter, another meeting was held on 16th April 1990, of the members of Delhi Urban Art Commission being the 602nd Meeting in which Mr. Abid Hussain–Chairman, Mr. P. P Shrivastava–member, Mr. Ravindra Bhan - member, Mr. Sharat Das–Member, Mr. Ashok Khosla - member, Mr. M. B Saxena - Secretary, Mr. D. D Madan - Officer, Mr. R. Vaidya - Architect Planner, Mr. Vinod Kumar - Deputy Architect were present and the layout plan for General pool Housing at Pinjrapole was considered and the minutes were recorded:

The proposal in the last meeting had informally been discussed at a preliminary conceptual stage, at the behest of Mr. P. P Shrivastava, a member as brought before the commission by the Central Public Works Department, and the other alternative by HUDCO's Consultant (Mr. Jasbir Sawhney) when certain observations were made. The layout plan forwarded by the Municipal Corporation of

Delhi (TP Department) was examined, and it was noted the proposal comprises 46 blocks of type IV, V, and VI with height varying from 4 to 12 stories including a hostel block resulting in 1454 dwelling units having spread over an area of 71.2 acres (including a Community Center). It was noted out of the above, there is a provision for 256 units planned in 4 stories, and a hostel block 8 stories with 105 units for the forthcoming Afro Asian Games.

The proposal noted the proposal of the 256 units submitted by the Central Public Works Department required relaxation regarding height, and otherwise, it fulfilled the Master plan, zonal plan, and other regulatory norms, including bye-laws, etc. In view of the urgency of the project, it was decided to clear the immediate requirements of the type IV quarters facing marshal Tito Marg by approving it as a 1st phase to be constructed by the Central Public Works Department, subject to two no. of blocks appearing isolated on the North-West side being re-adjusted, within part layout approved and the rest of the project, it was considered given its magnitude and importance required further in-depth study and inputs despite planning and landscaping.

It shows Delhi Urban Art Commission still rejected the conceptual proposal of HUDCO, but the proposal of the Central Public Works Department for 256 flats to be constructed for the Government was approved as it was as per Zonal Plan and Master Plan.

Mr. Rakesh Mehta, Director (Land), Ministry of Urban Development, addressed the difficulty on 23rd April 1990 to the Secretary Delhi Urban Art Commission, Mr. Saxena, that the urban design at a conceptual stage of 70 Acres of L&DO Land in Pinjrapole near Andrews Ganj on Khelgaon forwarded Urban Development is forwarded for consideration of Delhi Urban Art Commission. Since it is a time-bound project, Delhi Urban Art Commission may kindly consider it on a priority basis. Final submission through the Municipal Corporation of Delhi will be delivered shortly.
The Author's opinion here is the procedure was to submit the layout plan for approvals to the Municipal Corporation of Delhi, who would forward to the Town Planner, Municipal Corporation of Delhi for his comments, and on such approval, the layout would be forwarded to Delhi Urban Art Commission for their consideration. But all these procedures were bi passed for Andrew Ganj's land. It

is important to observe that the Urban Design of Pinjrapole area now Andrews Ganj was only submitted for conceptual approval, and they could submit no building plans before approval of the layout plan.

By now, HUDCO had already lost some portion, as it was given to the Central Public Works Department to construct 256 houses on part of the land, as the Central Public Works Department followed all the laws and master plan uses.

In pursuance to a letter dated 26th April 1990 of HUDCO to Mr. M. B Saxena, Secretary, Delhi Urban Art Commission regarding Urban Design of Andrews Ganj, prepared by HUDCO submitting the drawings demarcating the area of 256 houses of Central Public Works Department approved by Delhi Urban Art Commission, inquired on 30th April 1990 from Additional Town Planner (Land), Municipal Corporation of Delhi regarding layout plan for general pool housing for sports authority of India. Secretary, Delhi Urban Art Commission reiterated the minutes of the meeting dated 16th April 1990, and the observations made for further necessary action regarding Town Planner's letter number 1/48/49/89/TP/Municipal Corporation of Delhi/947/90, dated 15th March 1990, as in the proposal it was noted required relaxation regarding height, and otherwise, it fulfilled the Master plan, zonal plan and other regulatory norms, including bye-laws, etc.

There was a requirement of approval by the Land and Development Officer as well, but that was also passed in the garb of the fact that at present only conceptual approval is being sought, as Mr. Rakesh Mehta, Director (Land)-cum-L&DO, Ministry of Urban Development, in his communication dated 14th May 1990 informed Chairman, Delhi Urban Art Commission HUDCO has submitted the proposal of Urban Design Form at the conceptual stage for the Community Center at Pinjrapole. The proposal submitted by HUDCO was forwarded. The designs superseded the Designs already submitted by the Central Public Works Department earlier. It was mentioned that the approval of L&DO at this stage is unnecessary, and the same would be given only after the Delhi Urban Arts Commission has only approved the final drawings.

Being upset with the Central Public Works Department, HUDCO's Chairman, and S.K. Sharma informed on 16th May 1990 to Joint Secretary (Land), Mr. K. Dharmarajan, that HUDCO's Architect has reported that Central Public

Works Department has started work on 13.5 acres of Pinjrapole land as per the Urban Design prepared by HUDCO, while Central Public Works Department is to accommodate 256 houses in 10 acres earmarked by HUDCO. If this is permitted, the entire Urban Design will get dislocated, which may be inspected, and appropriate action may be taken.

The demarcated drawing of 10 acres of land to Central Public Works Department for 256 units for Afro Asian Games:

Mr. Rakesh Mehta, Director (Land)–L&DO, Ministry of Urban Development, on the request of HUDCO, confirmed on 18th May 1990 that allotment of land at Andrews Ganj to HUDCO is still under consideration, but HUDCO was authorized to start construction in the area and submit plans to Delhi Urban Art Commission and Delhi Municipal Corporation. This has become necessary given the urgency of the Afro Asian Games to be held in 1992. This authorization shall be valid until 31st December 1990.

Chapter: Seven

Mr. Murasoli Maran, Minister of Urban Development, the Government of Mr. V. P. Singh,

Ongoing through the records by me of Andrews Ganj, my view as the author is that it seems the Minister of Urban Development Mr. Murasoli Maran, under the Government of Mr. V. P. Singh, was unaware or was not informed of the constructions going on by HUDCO at Andrews Ganj with no allotment for HUDCO, due to which the Minister showed the concern for the development of flats for the officers of the Government. With no sanctions and no approvals, the Ministry informed Orally HUDCO to submit the layout plans and start construction as the Minister desired.

The Minister of Urban Development, Mr. Murasoli Maran, showed concern for constructing flats for Government Officers given the shortage of budgetary provisions. The Minister was concerned that the current year budget is only Rs. 35.52 Crores (US Dollar 21 million) for the whole of India. It has been possible to take up only 256 type IV quarters at Andrews Ganj, which are under construction by the Central Public Works Department for Rs. 10.52 Crores (US Dollar 6 million).

Mr. S.K. Sharma Chairman-cum-Managing Director HUDCO submitted in writing on 22nd May 1990 to Mr.

Srivastav Additional Secretary (Urban Development) regarding the development of housing in Andrews Ganj, and to get the project submitted a preliminary financial assessment of the proposal subject to cost benefits and tax implications. Further justifying that if we were to depend upon governmental budgetary support only, it is simply not possible to take up any additional construction on any appreciable scale, and an alternative way would have to be found.

Additional Secretary placed before the Minister that this matter was discussed with Chairman-cum-Managing Director, HUDCO, to explore possibilities of developing housing without budgetary support, using land as a resource. This would incidentally also allow HUDCO to show neighborhood cluster planning, which would benefit economies on land and building cost so effective building technologies in which the Ministry itself is deeply interested. Except for demonstration projects, HUDCO rarely takes up construction.

Chairman-cum-Managing Director HUDCO was sensible enough to take up this challenge and come up with a split project which could serve as a demonstration for improved design and technology in governmental housing construction, currently tied down with typical type designs and conventional technologies. We have discussed the scheme in great detail in several meetings. The Joint Secretary (Finance) has been good enough to examine the proposal. Principally, it was agreed HUDCO will invest its funds for the construction of houses and related neighborhood facilities on this land. The ministry will make available 17 acres of commercial land in Pinjrapole at a pre-determined market price for development. HUDCO will be free to license out parts of the development following an urban design by it and approved by all the Authorities.

Mr. D.R. Nakra, Chief Financial Officer of HUDCO, submitted on 24th May 1990 the layout plans with the letter dated 18th May 1990 of Mr. Ramesh Mehta, Director (Land)–L&DO, Ministry of Urban Development.

HUDCO's Chairman Mr. S.K. Sharma on 28th May 1990 addressed a letter to the Secretary that the Andrews Ganj project is important and would come in the Vigilance's purview Commission, and as HUDCO will use new technologies which are not scheduled for rates with the

Central Public Works Department, and hence there will be deviations. Please ensure our officers involved do not get into difficulties and may not get demoralized.

Mr. D.R. Nakra, Chief Financial Officer of HUDCO on 31st May 1990, submitted the building drawings which were not approved until the end of 1996 since they already cleared the buildings. Till now, the proposal was being discussed for 15 years to be given to HUDCO, the Andrews Ganj land, but unofficially HUDCO already had the possession of the land to carry on the developments at land.

HUDCO's Chairman-cum-Managing Director in its letter 31st May 1990 to the Secretary, Ministry of Urban Development complained about the Central Public Works Department building 256 houses on 9 acres, being the density of 28 units to an acre. HUDCO is building 1050 housing units in 25 acres, i.e., 42 units to an acre. HUDCO has suggested an alternative layout which was rejected by the Central Public Works Department. Considering the scarcity of land in Delhi, the prime location of Pinjrapole, and high land values, this is a permanent heavy loss to the Government of Rs. 10.00 Crores and 100 dwelling units.

In short, the view of the author is HUDCO did not want Central Public Works Department to get this 10-acre land and continued to complain against Central Public Works Department, who was working most diligently and honestly as per the fixed rates by the Government and as per the Master Plan and Zonal Development Plan of Zone F-3.

HUDCO on 5th June 1990 through Mr. P.S. Rana, Executive Director, submitted the sewerage, water supply, and storm water drains plan to the Municipal Corporation of Delhi, but these plans were finally not approved since HUDCO had built all these properties with no approvals of Municipal Corporation of Delhi with the consent of the Ministry of Urban Development Officers.

Town Planner, Municipal Corporation of Delhi informed HUDCO on 15th June 1990 in response to the drawings submitted by HUDCO on 24th May 1990, in which HUDCO had stated it was a time-bound project and be approved, to which he commented that various plans and documents submitted along with the application under reference are not complete as required under section 313 of the Delhi Municipal Corporation Act, 1957. Please furnish the following documents and other information at your earliest, so that further necessary action could be taken in the matter.

The important documents sought from HUDCO were the ownership documents to establish registered sale deed etc., and the Zonal development plan & Master Plan, 2001 be followed in the plan submitted for Community Center uses & housing, NOC from Civil Aviation, i.e., Airport Authority.

Was it not a scam that the illegal constructions carried on by HUDCO at Andrew Ganj were concealed from the Minister, Mr. Murasoli Maran, or that he was part of the scam?

Chapter: Eight

The Game of HUDCO Was on To Grab Andrews' Ganj Land

My dear readers, it shows the Minister, and the Secretary was kept happy by HUDCO's Chairman-cum-Managing Director, and all decisions were being made as per the liking of Mr. Sharma, the CMD. The Central Public Works Department was neglected, otherwise, the entire Andrews Ganj was to be developed by them or the Delhi Development Authority, as otherwise even HUDCO could not have been entrusted or given this land for allotment or development because of the Government policy guidelines.

It also shows, first, the land was being entrusted to HUDCO for development, but later HUDCO's Chairman-cum-Managing Director gave it away out to get the land leased for HUDCO. The game was on, and it is to be observed how the scam continues for this precious land, which every department or even the Prime Minister's Office was eyeing to develop university or any other institutions in the name of Prime Minister, for example, Indira Gandhi University.

I also gathered from the documents that HUDCO, having no title or any allotment, took possession of the land and named Andrews Ganj land HUDCO place, which made the public believe as if the entire land is owned by HUDCO.

The boards of HUDCO Place could be seen crossing the road where land was situated, informed to me by my friends in Delhi. The Ministry of Urban Development never objected to being named HUDCO Place at Andrews Ganj land. Now in correspondences, HUDCO started as HUDCO Place.

There was another meeting Minutes of 614th Meeting of the Delhi Urban Art Commission Held on July 20, 1990, when again all the same members were present the Layout Plan regarding Community Center, Zonal Park, General Pool Housing Pinjrapole (Preliminary concept) was discussed informally but not found satisfactory although Mr. Jasbir Sawhney highlighted the main features of the project which comprised a Community Center with a hotel 36 meter high, cultural center 150-meter height, Guesthouses clusters with 13.5-meter height, and shopping malls in structures ranging from 10.5 meters to 13.5-meter height as an area of 17.6 acres, with zonal green 18 acres, 60 number of type-VI unit in a 3 Storied development, 210 number of type V units in a 4 Storied development, 320 no. of type-IV units with a total area of pool housing 35.6 acres, all was as per Master Plan 2001.

On rejecting the proposal, Jasbir Sawhney was asked to further develop the proposal as per the observations and submit the same along with the proforma of planning permission and requisites documents and materials as per the Delhi Urban Art Commission guidelines, including a complete set of drawing of the three-dimensional model detailed project report, giving a critical analysis of the various components (area wise) for further consideration of the commission formally at the conceptual stage.

They also held discussions on 26th July 1990 in the office of Town Planner, Municipal Corporation of Delhi. Jasbir Sawhney was again advised of many points and agreed to incorporate them in the drawings and resubmit them again on 3rd August.

To grab the precious land in the heart of South Delhi at Andrews Ganj, S.K. Sharma, Chairman-cum-Managing Director, HUDCO suggested to Mr. PP Shrivastav, Additional Secretary, Ministry of Urban Development on 16th August 1990, which could not be suggested otherwise, but he did so by reminding of recalling the discussions with the Joint Secretary that the objectives of the Ministry will be best subserved if the approach stated below is adopted:

The ministry should keep the title over the 17-acre Community Center land in Pinjrapole, and make it available to HUDCO on a 32-year lease, with the stipulation that the land and assets developed thereon will vest in the Government on the expiry of the lease period. On the understanding that they would use the resources generated through the development for developing General Pool housing, we may allot the land to HUDCO on a nominal lease premium of Rupee one per annum. HUDCO will develop the land as per the approved urban design and license specified areas or built space for a period not exceeding 30 years, and use the resources generated for constructing central pool housing on the housing land available in Pinjrapole.

We may permit HUDCO to keep 10 percent of the resources generated. It may also be permitted to retain 5 to 10 percent of the housing for officials of HUDCO and other autonomous organizations under the Ministry. A committee will monitor the project, comprising Chairman-cum-Managing Director, HUDCO, Additional Secretary (Urban Development), and Joint Secretary, Finance. It should be possible for HUDCO to make available 1500 to 2000 houses for the central pool using the resources generated.

The architect Jasbir Sawhney on 9th August submitted the filled form to the Municipal Corporation of Delhi with a copy to Delhi Urban Art Commission for consideration of plans at the conceptual stage, putting in owner: Government of India and promoter: HUDCO.

On 1st August 1990, the Central Public Works Department again objected to the letter sent by the ministry referring to the letter of HUDCO that the Central Public Works Department and not HUDCO has planned the complete land in Pinjrapole. Accordingly, Central Public Works Department, Chief Architect, Mr. M.K. Rishi, detailed a letter dated 11th August 1990 addressed to the ministry the grievance that planning of 71.2 acres land at Andrews Ganj was to be developed by Central Public Works Department for the last decade. Just because the ministry allotted the land to societies, they decided we would keep 7 acres for a Community Center. But the matter went to the court, and this office prepared various alternatives to develop this land.

Now the Community Center is enlarged to 17 acres. This office further prepared the plans accordingly and presented them to the Delhi Urban Art Commission, and 256 type IV quarters were separated for the urgency of Afro Asian games to be completed in 1991 itself. Now the residential 10 acres have been reduced, as it has been proposed by HUDCO to have 17 acres for the Community Center. This office is unaware of which stage the Ministry of Urban Development took such a decision that HUDCO will now construct even 100 additional units.

In the process, HUDCO is cornered and unable to get the approvals. Now appears Chairman-cum-Managing Director HUDCO is asking to add 100 quarters as 5th and 6th floor in the four stories under construction. As regards Central Public Works Department is concerned, the proposal of the Central Public Works Department has the approval of the Delhi Urban Art Commission and the ministry, while HUDCO plans are not even approved at the conceptual stage.

This letter on 11th August of the Central Public Works Department was not responded to and kept in the cold storage, as it had no reply to give, as they knew the wrong decision was being made in favor of HUDCO at the behest of the Minister and the secretary.

Again, in another meeting of Delhi Urban Art Commission on 31st August 1990, the proposal was considered and rejected, which was informed to Jasbir Sawhney on 19th October 1990 with many observations regarding the location, and the bulk of the transit hostel block accommodating 390 units was still considered massive, creating congestion in the complex. Mr. Kamath, the Consultant of HUDCO for this block, who was present during the meeting, was advised to revise in such a manner that the distance between the Type-IV block clusters on either side is to be improved, and the same does not appear massive.

Certain specific suggestions were given to him for attempting a terracing concept, starting with more height towards the southeast side. Mr. Jasbir Sawhney, Architect of the layout scheme, was advised to look into the details of the various type designs (which required improvements) and to submit the same along with the scheme through the concerned local body for consideration of the Commission after the revised transit hostel block was approved from the Commission.

On 8th October 1990, HUDCO's executive director, Dr. P.S. Rana, appointed Integrated Project Management Group Pvt Limited, a company to submit building plans and follow-up same with all concerned Government departments like Municipal Corporation of Delhi (Municipal Corporation of Delhi), Delhi Development Authority (Delhi Development Authority), Delhi Urban Art Commission (Delhi Urban Art Commission), DESU (Delhi Electricity Supply Unit), DGCA (Director General Civil Aviation), MTNL (Mahanagar Telephone Nigam Limited, DFS (Delhi Fire Services), etc. in respect Andrews Ganj land, and they named it HUDCO Place as if they owned the subject land by now.

My dear readers, the 90s had already started when HUDCO's scam started by getting the Andrews Ganj Land in the garb of that land entrusted to HUDCO to develop for the Government. Sometimes the stand was taken, the Government is the owner of the land.

Let's rewind to the 50s when the entire plot was being structured. The year was 1950 when the Andrews Ganj land was allotted to Pinjrapole Society for 10 years at Rs. 25,000 (US Dollar 2021) lease fee. After the eviction of the land by the order of the Supreme Court in 1985, the same Andrews Ganj land was allotted to Societies belonging to Members of Parliament and the Government Officers, which was again evicted by the Supreme Court in 1989 by directing the Government to pay back the monies received with interest to the Societies.

Then came HUDCO again, another scam started by building illegal constructions at the behest of the Government. But who is to be held responsible, and when will they be held responsible? The help of the Government continued HUDCO to encourage the ongoing illegal construction with no approval of the local bodies, and contrary to the laws of the city and the country. The activities of construction by HUDCO started in 1989-1990 to be completed in 1991 in the need of the Afro Asian Games to be held, which were canceled later.

Chapter: Nine

Another Scam of Andrews Ganj Land Started

When the Minister, Mr. Murasoli Maran, under the Prime Ministership of Mr. V.P. Singh, the Land-use of Andrews Ganj 71 acres was notified on 1st August 1990 in the New Master Plan, 2001 for using the Convention Center for Institutions. This was notified on the approval of the Minister of Urban Development, Mr. Murasoli Maran when the entire ministry was aware of the ongoing constructions by HUDCO at Andrews Ganj in the garb of the urgency of the Afro Asian Games.

The documents show this resolution passed by Delhi Development Authority meant that any plan sanctioned before 1st August 1990 where no change of land use is involved and a prescribed building plan fee had been paid before 1st August 1990 will be per relevant master plan provisions i.e., Master Plan Delhi,1962. But in the present case of Andrews Ganj land, no plans were submitted before 1st August 1990, along with the fee which could be under the old Master Plan, i.e., Master Plan for Delhi, 1962. The Andrews Ganj land use as per Master Plan for Delhi, 2001 was for Convention Center, but HUDCO continued to develop and construct the buildings as per Master Plan for Delhi, 1962.

Even the construction carried out by the Central Public Works Department on 10 acres of land at Andrews Ganj had the approval of the layout plan by the Delhi Urban Art Commission, but did not have the approval of building plans from the Municipal Corporation of Delhi. The entire construction of 256 flats had been carried out with no approval in anticipation of the approval in the future, as the constructions were carried out for the Government of India.

Dear readers, it shows in India that if the constructions are for the Government, then the building laws are not applicable as if they only apply to the public. The notion is erroneous, and the constructions carried out without the building sanctions are normally demolished by the Municipal Corporation of Delhi, but in the present case, no action was taken, being afraid of the Ministry.
As the author, there is no doubt of a fraction, even that the constructions by HUDCO were already being carried out since the last few months in the name of HUDCO Place, with no allotment in their favor by the Land & Development Officer. HUDCO in connivance with the Ministry constructed unauthorized buildings with no sanctions of Municipal Corporation of Delhi of building plans, nor was the approval of the Fire Department neither

the approval of the Delhi Urban Art Commission obtained. HUDCO and Ministry knew well that the approvals from all concerned Government departments, like Municipal Corporation of Delhi, Delhi Development Authority, Delhi Urban Art Commission, Delhi Electricity Supply Undertaking, Mahanagar Telephone Nigam Limited, Delhi Fire Services, etc., were compulsorily required.

As advised by the Chairman-cum-Managing Director of HUDCO, the Ministry of Urban Development through the Under Secretary put up for approval of the Joint Secretary, Secretary, Joint Secretary Finance, and the Minister for sanctioning the allotment of prime Andrews Ganj land measuring 42.6 acres @ Re. 1/- per acre for 32 years lease and 17 acres green land with no charges to the Land & Development Officer of the Ministry. The approval was granted by the Ministry of Mr. V.P. Singh, who was Prime Minister when the Urban Development Minister was Mr. Murasoli Maran, as the Ministry changed on 10th November 1990, i.e., within 9 days of the letter resulting in a scam of Andrews Ganj land.

On the advice of Chairman-cum-Managing Director, HUDCO, the precious land of Andrews Ganj could be allotted to the Land & Development Officer for Housing & Urban Development Corporation Limited (HUDCO). The entire approval was obtained hurriedly, as there was already news that Prime Minister Mr. V.P. Singh resigned as the support of various parties was being withdrawn.

The readers would believe the truth that the cost of the land measuring 42.6 acres plus green land of 17 acres was more than Rs.200 crores (US Dollar 114.28 million), but 42.6 acres were given at Rs. 1/- per acre to Land & Development Office to allot to HUDCO for a 32-year lease. There were many controversies due to which the Land & Development Officer did not issue the allotment to HUDCO. But HUDCO continued to construct illegally the entire complex, and the Ministry was in total knowledge of illegal constructions being carried out by HUDCO.
The reality behind such hurried decision was that these approvals of such allotment of land to Land & Development Officer to allot the land to HUDCO were to overcome the difficulties of the constructions already carried out by HUDCO with no allotment in their favor, and the Minister advised there was an urgency of Afro Asian Games due to which HUDCO is already constructing the buildings, and at present, the allotment is being issued

only to Land & Development Officer, who instead of such approval will be advised not to issue any allotment letter to HUDCO until further instructions.

It is interesting to note my dear readers that the Ministry of Urban Development Officers and the Minister of Urban Development, Mr. Murasoli Maran, was well aware that Andrews Ganj land was preferred for Convention Center and for Development of Institutions, which was notified with the support of the Prime Minister, Mr. V.P. Singh. But on 1st August 1990, when the Master Plan 2001 was notified, none of them knew the Government would go away this year itself. So, another scam of Andrews Ganj land resulted in another disaster of this precious land.

Chapter: Ten

Allotment of Andrews Ganj Land to Land & Development Office For 32 Years Lease for HUDCO

It is on record to note the land use of Andrews Ganj 71 acres was not for residential or for the development of the Community Center. The Officers of the Ministry of Urban Development hurriedly covered up their mistakes, took the approval from the Minister sanctioning Andrews Ganj land 71 acres for allotment to Land & Development Officer for HUDCO.

Immediately on the same day of the approval by the Minister, the allotment letter for 42.6 acres at Andrews Ganj for 32 years lease was issued on 1st November 1990 by the Government of India to the Land Division of the Ministry of Urban Development, signed by Under Secretary to the Government of India, Mr. K. K. Gupta for HUDCO.

17.6 acres of land for a Community Center be leased on payment of a token premium of rupee one, and annual ground rent of rupee one per acre for a 32-year lease.

25.0 acres of residential land will be leased for 10 years on payment of a token premium of rupee one and annual ground rent of rupee one per acre. After the expiry of this period, the land along with structures to be erected by

HUDCO thereon will revert to the Ministry of Urban Development.

The land for the Community Center should be utilized for the development of hostel and guesthouse facilities, conference hall, shopping, and other Community Center facilities, as per the urban design for the complex approved by this Ministry.

HUDCO will complete the construction of the Afro Asian Games Authorities to use temporarily at least 100 houses /flats before these games are held in 1990-91.

We entrust 18 acres of land to HUDCO without payment of any fee for care and maintenance. As Zonal Green, HUDCO develops this area and maintains it until further directions from the Government. HUDCO may charge the cost of development and maintenance of the Zonal green to the accounts of the Community Center project.

A review/monitoring Committee comprising Additional Secretary, Joint Secretary dealing with the subject, and Joint Secretary (Finance) from the Ministry of Urban Development and Chairman-cum-Managing Director,

HUDCO will monitor/review the implementation of this project and will function as an Empowered Committee to take investment and disposal decisions as may be necessary for efficient completion of 'the project. Company Secretary, HUDCO will function as Secretary of this Committee.

The details of leasing arrangements regarding facilities developed on the Community Center land will be intimated in due course.

This issues with the concurrence of the Finance Division vide their U.O. No. 1724/ (F) dated 1st November 1990. The Joint Secretary, Mr. K. Dharmarajan, on 9th November 1990, who had taken a keen interest in getting the approval to give the land to HUDCO, informed HUDCO it is a time-bound action plan which will be sent at the earliest to follow up the scheme and regular review by the Monitoring Committee set up, and the first meeting of the Monitoring Committee will be called immediately to discuss the decision to be taken on various action points for expediting the project.

On 10th November 1990, Prime Minister Mr. Vishwanath Pratap Singh was thrown out, and all the parties supported

Mr. Chandra Shekhar to be the next Prime Minister who took an oath on 10th November 1990 as Prime Minister of India. The entire Ministry had to change, as all the Ministers of Mr. V.P. Singh had to resign. The new Prime Minister, Mr. Chander Shakhar, appointed Mr. Daulat Ram Saran as the Minister of Urban Development, who took charge on 21st November 1990 and shuffled all the officers in a month, appointing Mr. R.V. Pillai, Additional Secretary, Mr. PSA Sundram, Chairman-cum-Managing Director, HUDCO, and Mr. B. Bhattacharya, Joint Secretary (Finance), but retained Mr. K. Dharmarajan, Joint Secretary.

In the meeting held by Delhi Development Authority (Zonal Plan Section), Mr. Surendera Srivastava, Deputy Director (Zonal Planner), prepared various regulations required under the provisions under Master Plan for Delhi, 2001, considering for claiming rule & regulations framed earlier required modification under the provision of Master Plan, 2001 for hotels, boarding houses, Guesthouses, hostels, lodging houses and motels (building standards), which were placed for approval on 21st November 1990.

It was decided that Development Controls/Zoning Regulations of the Master plan were notified on 1st August

1990, and applicability on the building plans submitted before the date of notification File No. F.20 (20)/89/M.P.): After the coming into force of the Master Plan for Delhi, 2001 from 1st August 1990, the matter about approval of cooperative group housing society layout plans/building plans was discussed in the meeting of the Technical Committee held on 31st August 1990, and the Resolution has been passed:

Resolved that as a one-time measure of administrative convenience, and by liberal interpretation of the Master Plan, all pending building plans for construction on individual residential plots, institutional plots, and plots allotted to group housing societies, which were submitted to Delhi Development Authority before 1st August 1990, be finalized and approved as per relevant Master Plan provisions in force at the time of submission, as a special case, subject to the following conditions:
That such plot is part of a regular layout plan already sanctioned by the competent authority. It does not involve any change in prescribed land use. That they have paid the prescribed building plan fee before 1st August 1990. That conversion of lease charges under the terms of the lease (as for the plots located in the NDMC area) is not involved. A

list of such pending cases should be prepared and furnished to the Vice-Chairman, Delhi Development Authority, within one month.

Mr. P.S. Rana, Executive Director, HUDCO informed on 21st November 1990 to Mr. S C Gupta, Director (Planning), Delhi Development Authority, referring to a letter dated 15th November 1990 of HUDCO regarding a project entrusted by the Ministry to HUDCO. The review and monitoring committee has been postponed to be held on 26th November 1990 at Noon in the office of Chairman-cum-Managing Director, HUDCO submitting that the agenda would be to discuss Pinjrapole project (Andrews Ganj) being time-bound for completion. The Andrews Ganj project consists of the construction of a Guesthouse, residential flats of officer categories, transit flats, swimming pool, shop, nursery school, etc.

Further, the brief status of progress was discussed in the meeting regarding the work for the construction of a guesthouse in Cluster A & B, which was awarded to the contractors on 25th October 1990. As per the terms of conditions, Phase-1 of the Clusters is to be completed by 15th October 1991 in every respect. The tendered cost of the preliminary cost of Rs.18 crores (US Dollar 10.28 million). The approval from the Delhi Urban Art Commission/Municipal Corporation of Delhi for building plans is being persuaded by the project Management Consultants / Architects.

Since the buildings were being constructed by the Central Public Works Department also without approval of the building plans, Mr. P. Krishnan, Chief Engineer, Central Public Works Department, requested the Additional Secretary, Mr. P.P. Shrivastav, Ministry of Urban Development on 22nd November 1990 that the Municipal Corporation of Delhi authorities has raised various objections regarding the layout and building drawings about Type IV quarters at Pinjrapole, which are to be used for the Afro Asian Games. They have furnished all the necessary clarifications to them. Given the insufficient time left, we had to take up this work also in anticipation of formal approval by the Municipal Corporation of Delhi. I shall be grateful if you could use your good offices with the Municipal Corporation of Delhi to expedite the approval of the drawing so that we do not face my difficulties at a later date.

The building section of Municipal Corporation of Delhi issued an office order dated 21st December 1990 confirming the decision of the Delhi Development Authority made on 21st November 1990 that in the meeting of the Building Plan Committee held on 4th December 1990, it was decided the matter regarding disposal of building plans submitted before 1st August 1990, i.e. prior to the enforcement of Master Plan, 2001, was discussed, and it was decided based on minutes of the Ministry of Urban Development that these plans should be sanctioned on the norms prevailing prior to the enforcement of Master Plan, 2001.

It is interesting to note the Ministry of Urban Development made such a decision, thinking of Andrews Ganj's land, the norms of the Master Plan for Delhi, 1962 would apply to this land, while the land use of Andrews Ganj had changed to the Convention Center, which was not being considered in view of the decision that HUDCO had applied for sanctions of building plans and layout plans prior to 1st August 1990. The factual part is HUDCO had not applied for approval of the building plans prior to 1st August 1990, and such stipulation did not apply to Andrews Ganj land.

Was it not a Scam Mr. Murasoli Maran, Minister of Urban Development, approved the allotment to the Land & Development Office of Andrews Ganj land, just 9 days before his resignation as a Minister, and the resignation of the Prime Minister Mr. V. P. Singh?

Chapter: Eleven

HUDCO Manipulated the Books of Accounts regarding Andrew Ganj Land, which Has Escaped the Eyes of Comptroller Auditor General of India (CAG)

The Scam is clear of Andrews Ganj land since there was no approval of layout plan nor the building plans were approved, but the contractors were told to go ahead with the constructions, as they are Government buildings and Municipal Corporation of Delhi cannot come and demolish. This was the attitude of the officers and HUDCO as if they had no laws to be followed, and as if they made these laws for the public only. The scam of Andrews Ganj land continued to get deeper and deeper since even the Chartered Accountants of HUDCO objected the incomes will be taxable as applicable, but HUDCO did not bother to follow any accountancy procedure for Andrews Ganj land.

HUDCO had awarded the civil works of Guesthouses cluster A and B at Andrews Gang in October 1990 to M/s Shapoorji Pallonji & Co. and M/s Ahluwalia Contracts India Limited informing that the conceptual designs prepared by the interior designers have been approved, and they have been advised to prepare their mock-up rooms. The contractors constructed the buildings as per target to be completed in October 1991, although unofficially the buildings were already under construction by these contractors before the awards.

The layout plan submitted by HUDCO was taken up, and the Town Planner, Municipal Corporation of Delhi on 9th January 1991 informed Chief Finance, HUDCO regarding Pinjrapole, Andrews Gang that the mentioned proposal was submitted to this office u/s 313 of the DMC Act, 1957. We issued an invalid notice vide this office letter dated 15th June 1990 for certain compliances. However, your architect has however far made no compliances/other until now. This case has also been discussed in the meeting held on 18th December 1990, and it has been desired a representative from your office or architect be asked to attend the coming meeting, held in the conference room of Finance Head, Charter Building at Connaught Place every Tuesday at 9.30 am to explain the scheme in person.
In the layout committee meeting held on 22nd January 1991, they again rejected the layout plans submitted by HUDCO of Andrews Ganj land.

HUDCO had submitted on 13th January 1991 the layout plans of Andrews Ganj land to Deputy Director Mr. Anil Barai, Delhi Development Authority (Master Planning), who sought clarification on 25th January 1991 addressed to the Chief Architect, Central Public Works Department, and Mr. P.S. Rana, Executive Director, HUDCO regarding

Construction at Andrews Gang, New Delhi to send a copy of layout plan duly showing the total area of the scheme and surrounding areas, submitted to Municipal Corporation of Delhi for approval Here, the change of land use is involved. As per Master Plan for Delhi, 2001, the site is earmarked for 'Convention Center' (Public & Semi-public facilities), due to which the Master Planning Section of Delhi Development Authority also rejected the layout plans.

Town Planner asked HUDCO, Municipal Corporation of Delhi on 12th February 1991 regarding layout plan at Pinjrapole, Andrews Gang informing that the proposal submitted by HUDCO has been considered in a layout committee meeting held on 22nd January 1991, and accordingly HUDCO was requested to submit the layout plans should include the requesting community facility sites as per Master Plan, 2001 regarding primary/nursery school, community hall, E.S.S., C.S., etc., and separate permission of personal visit of the officer. Delhi Electricity Supply Undertaking has approved ESS sites, no objection certificate from civil aviation for multistoried hostels.

Mr. Anil Barai, Deputy Director, Delhi Development Authority (Master Planning), again reminded HUDCO regarding HUDCO's letter on 13th February 1991 on the subject of Andrews Ganj land informing them he is a director Mr. Anil Barai, Dy. Director (MP), Delhi Development Authority, who had requested on 28th January 1991 to send a copy of the layout plan with the total proposals measuring 71.0 areas duly authenticated, so that the case could be processed further.

HUDCO's Statutory Chartered Accountant, Mr. K.S. V.S. Manian, a Partner, V. Sankar Aiyar & Co., objected to the way the Andrews Ganj was being reflected in the books of account in forming HUDCO on 12th February 1991 to Mr. Raghavan, Chief (finance), HUDCO. It is noted the Government of India has allotted land on a lease basis for a different purpose, as stated below to HUDCO.

- **Community Center construction on 17.6 Acres**
- **Residential Houses on 25.0**
- **Additional Green Area 18.0**

Total 60.6

The land of the Community Center is leased to HUDCO on a token payment for Rs.1 per acre, and annual ground rent of Rs.1 per Acre covering 32 years lease. The residential land is allotted on a leased basis for 10 years on a token payment of a premium of Re.1 per acre. As per the note, it is noted the green area of 18 acres of land is stated to be only entrusted to HUDCO for developing and maintaining the same until further orders from the Government.
From the note, it is clear HUDCO must develop these projects on its own with its funds, and then build them through its contractor, etc., over the period. HUDCO is permitted to dispose of the constructed premises on 17.6 acres, i.e., the Community Center, and the fund should be utilized for the construction of Central Government general pool housing on 25 acres of land.

In our opinion, the whole thing is an adventure in trade, i.e., business transactions and business activity. The profits resulting from the sale of the buildings will be business income, which would be earned over a period by selling the various buildings constructed by HUDCO. Therefore, that can be accounted for based on an accounting policy existing with the company, reproduced as below:

Work in progress is valued by taking actual cost incurred plus profit allocated based on a percentage of completion method:

- **Up to completion of 25% No profit**
- **Above 25% till completion 80% of the estimated profit**
- **On completion of the job balance of the 100% profit**

The figures, however, given in the note, about the cost and the sale price, and the profits are only understood as provisional figures. It may also be noted that the estimated surplus of Rs. 16 crores (US Dollar 7 million) are thus the expected profit, and that will be accounted for over a period in different years on the accounting policy in the profit-and-loss account of HUDCO.

Therefore, as HUDCO now is not having any exemption from income tax, the profit resulting and accounted for is subject to income tax at the rates prevailing in the respective years, when the profit arising from the sale of these buildings is declared as per the accounting policy in the respective years in the profit-and-loss account.

Dear readers, the Scam by HUDCO is also by HUDCO manipulated the books of accounts without following the advice of Chartered Accountants, which also escaped the eyes of Comptroller and Auditor General of India (CAG), which is mandatory to be conducted of the public sector companies by CAG, as CAG has reported many frauds in the public sectors, but such a big scam by HUDCO went scot-free from the eyes of CAG as well.

CAG had brought into the limelight the Indian government's much-publicized Special Economic Zone (SEZ) policy, which had drastically failed in achieving its objectives of generating additional economic activity, creation of employment opportunities, development of infrastructure facilities, among others. Instead, the policy had become a profitable business for private developers who had been raising loans or mortgaging the gained land. Even the Comptroller Auditor General of India (CAG) trashed the SEZ policy, claiming how the land acquired from poor farmers was being sold at a market price and converted into real estate.

Was it not a Scam that the Comptroller Auditor General of India (CAG) omitted to catch in HUDCO's balance sheet?

Chapter: Twelve

Scam in Purchases by HUDCO For Andrews Ganj Project by Not Following Government Department Fixed Prices

My observations as an author regarding Scam by HUDCO regarding the Andrews Ganj project are various violations. As in the Government sector, the rates for individual items for construction are fixed by the Central Public Works Department, which must be followed by every department to prevent corruption in the purchases and the contracts to be entered with the builders. But HUDCO did not follow Central Public Works Department rates, which made it immune to making money in the purchases and contracts by the officers of HUDCO. Chairman-cum-Managing Director of HUDCO bypassed all these rates in the garb of the quality of construction cannot be ensured with the rates of the Central Public Works Department, and that in the project there are certain items for which there are no rates prescribed in the Central Public Works Department schedule.

HUDCO and Ministry of Urban Development Officers remained hand in glove regarding Andrews Ganj Project, while the area of concern was discussed in the Empowered Committee to monitor the Andrews Ganj project, but nowhere the Committee discussed the sanctions of layout plans or the building plans for the constructions proceeded on, which violates the building bylaws and other laws.

As per terms of allotment dated 1st November 1990 of Andrews, Ganj land was for 32 years' lease by the Government to Land & Development Officer for further allotment to HUDCO. The terms specially stipulated that 17.6 Acres of land for the Community Center will be released on payment of a token premium of rupee one and annual ground rent of rupee one per acre for a 32-year lease, which was even discussed in the Empowered Committee, specially created for the Andrews Ganj project. The Empowered Committee comprised Government Officers, and HUDCO Officers knew that the lease premium fixed was not paid, and Land & Development had not yet issued the allotment of Andrews Ganj land to HUDCO, but they let the constructions go on jointly knowingly that they were illegal.

The Under the Secretary Ministry of Urban Development requested on 6th March 1991 to Delhi Development Authority (Master Planning) publish the notification as the amendment of the hotel, motel, guest lodging boarding houses in the regulations, 1977 out no notification has been published, only motel's amendment was published/notified vide this notification dated 27.5.1989. In pursuance, Delhi Development Authority on 1st April 1991 considered whether these amendments are necessary, as per Master

Plan for Delhi, 2001, which was notified on 1st August 1990.

There were various disputes which had arisen between the Central Public Works Department and HUDCO, as the plans of the Central Public Works Department were approved by the Municipal Corporation of Delhi, but the layout plan of HUDCO was not yet approved, due to which Central Public Works Department on 6th May 1991 officially wrote to Mr. K.S. Batra, Project Coordinator, Pinjrapole HUDCO project the roads being constructed are not as per the layout plan approved by Municipal Corporation of Delhi. The officers of the Central Public Works Department had met Dr. P.S. Rana, Executive Director, on 30th April 1991 and 1st May 1991 that the matter may be sorted out. It was advised to attend a coordination meeting on 2nd May 1991, and it was explained in the meeting to Mr. Jasbir Sawhney, Architect, as well as HUDCO's officers. It was, therefore, requested to take necessary action for modifications in HUDCO's layout plan.

The Delhi Development Authority decided that as the Master Plan for Delhi 2001 has come into force since 1st

August 1990, the amendments as desired by the Ministry are not required to be processed, which was informed on 14th May 1991 to the Under Secretary. Under Secretary to the Ministry of Urban Development again reiterated on 29th May 1991, seeking a point-wise reply to the issues raised by the Ministry on 8th February 1990, but Delhi Development Authority (Master Planning) declined to reply.

The company Secretary of HUDCO, Gopal Krishan confirmed the minutes on 5th April 1991 to all the members of Review and monitoring empowered committee first meeting held on 15th March 1991 on the Andrews Ganj land, the present members were Mr. SK Sharma Chairman-cum-Managing Director HUDCO in (Chair), Mr. RV Pillai Additional Secretary (Delhi) Ministry of Urban Development, Mr. PSA Sundaram Joint Secretary (EH) Ministry of Urban Development, Mr. B Bhattacharya Joint Secretary (Finance) Ministry of Urban Development, Mr. K Dharmarajan Joint Secretary (Land) Ministry of Urban Development, Mr. Mulkh Raj Director Finance, HUDCO, Mr. Gopal Krishan Company Secretary HUDCO. As suggested by Chairman-cum-Managing Director, it was decided that during the initial periods of the project, the

Committee should meet in the third week of monthly. It was pointed out that the scope of the committee is only to review and monitor the project at Andrews Ganj.

It was pointed out by the members that as required under the items & conditions of the allotment of the plot, detailed estimates of the project should be prepared. This was necessary to monitor escalation in the cost of the project and to avoid adverse comments. Chairman-cum-Managing Director HUDCO pointed out it was not appropriate to adopt the Central Public Works Department rates because if this is done, the quality of construction cannot be ensured. Further, in the project, there are certain items for which there are no rates prescribed in the Central Public Works Department schedule. It was decided that Director (Finance) HUDCO will prepare a note on the various options available for the disposal of the properties for consideration of the committee.

Chairman-cum-Managing Director, HUDCO also pointed out that at present there was no definite indication whether the Afro-Asian-Games were to be held or not. If the games were not to be held, then there was no need to rush the project under pressure, since it will lead to increased cost of construction. It was decided that the Ministry of Urban Development should take up this matter with the Secretary (Sports) and written confirmation as to the holding of the games should be obtained.

The company Secretary of HUDCO, Gopal Krishan confirmed the minutes on 8th May 1991 to all the members of Review and monitoring empowered committee's second meeting held on 19th April 1991 on the progress to be reviewed of Andrews Ganj land, the present members were Mr. SK Sharma Chairman-cum-Managing Director HUDCO in (Chair), Mr. RV Pillai Additional Secretary (Delhi) Ministry of Urban Development, Mr. PSA Sundarm Joint Secretary (EH) Ministry of Urban Development, Mr. B Bhattacharya Joint Secretary (Finance) Ministry of Urban Development, Mr. K Dharmarajan Joint Secretary (L&I) Ministry of Urban Development, Mr. Mulkh Raj Director Finance, HUDCO, Mr. Gopal Krishan Company Secretary HUDCO.

Chairman-cum-Managing Director HUDCO had pointed out it was not appropriate to adopt the Central Public Works Department rates, because if this is done, the quality of construction cannot be ensured. Further, in the project, there are certain items for which there are no rates prescribed in the Central Public Works Department schedules appearing in the 1st paragraph of the previous minutes. Administrative approvals are substituted.

Chairman-cum-Managing Director HUDCO suggested it will be ideal if actual disposal of property is undertaken by the L&DO. He also referred to the recent notices received from implications, which can be as high as Rs 2 crores per year. Seeing the tax incidence, it will be better if the Ministry of Urban Development cancels the allotment of HUDCO and re-allots it at the time of disposal. The Director of Finance referred to the implication of condition 2 (ii) of the allotment letter, under which land has been transferred to HUDCO. The condition needs to be modified so that actual costs of maintenance and tax are paid by the Ministry of Urban Development.

It was discussed in the meeting at item no. 2.2 that the terms of sanction vide OM No. J- 13014/6/90-LD dated the 1st November 1990 to Land & Development Officer by the Ministry of Urban Development specifically stipulates that 17.6 Acres of land for a Community Center will be released on payment of a token premium of rupee one and annual ground rent of rupee one per acre for 32 years. The land for the Community Center should be utilized for the development of hostel and guesthouse facilities conference hall, shopping, and other Community Center facilities as per the urban design for the complex approved by this Ministry.

The Chairman-cum-Managing Director submitted the Objective of HUDCO in Implementing this project was the two objectives that motivated the development of HUDCO place were to promote quality of urban design / up-to-date construction management system to make available accommodation to certain professional groups at affordable rates and to raise resources for financing staff housing for central Government employees. For HUDCO, it is not only a commercial venture to give a 15 percent net rate of return on its investment, but also an opportunity to convert its design ideas into reality and offer its residents a place with a traditional ambiance and modern facilities.

The Scam by HUDCO in constructing on Andrews Ganj land for not following Central Public Works Department fixed rates of procurement of the materials is also evident. The scam by HUDCO in respect of Andrew Ganj's land was well-known to the Empowered Committee, including HUDCO, that they will be eligible to pay income tax, as advised by HUDCO's Chartered Accountants, but the same was deliberately ignored.

Was it not a Scam to evade Income Tax and Property Tax by a company that was liable for Income Tax legally on the interest being earned?

The Empowered Committee was aware that the disposal of these properties should be handled by the Land & Development office in the Ministry of Urban Development, who had extensive experience in real estate, but everything was ignored intentionally and deliberately.

In the second Empowered Committee held on 19th April 1991 to monitor Andrews Ganj's project named by HUDCO as HUDCO Place, the description of properties was placed and discussed.

It was finalized that the development will be a Unique Urban Experience consisting of a large plaza for social interaction, cultural center Executive club, basera for low budget tourist hotel, air-conditioned shopping mall polyclinic, restaurants, shop art galleries on the street, open court, and vast landscaped green. These properties will be disposed of in the open market. In the first phase, it is proposed to commission the Guesthouses, with all essential infrastructure being made available by October 1991, when Asian games are likely to be held. In the second phase, it is proposed to complete the construction of an arcade, cultural block, etc. It is proposed to complete phase it by October 1992.

The site for the 12-story hotel and shopping mall can be auctioned at any time, but it will be better to synchronize it with the beginning by phase II. In any case, these plots can be auctioned only after some basic development regarding services has been done.

A complete financial feasibility report needs to be prepared in respect of each element so that the stakes involved in each alternative set of decisions are clear. This shall account for the cost of construction (including interest), overhead costs, any, and the surplus expected if the disposal must be undertaken through HUDCO. The tax implication of it must be taken into account, as advised by our tax consultant (i.e., Sankar Aiyar, a copy of which was circulated to all the members of the Empowered Committee).

It was discussed in the Empowered Committee to monitor Andrews Ganj's project that each element of the property needs not be taken as a profit center, yet one cannot sideline the basic objective of making the project cost-effective and manage the disposal in a manner that maximum surplus is generated for additional pool housing. Options for Disposal were discussed: Guesthouse lumps.

The guest houses will be managed like a hotel. There are various options to dispose of this property. One option is to auction the Guesthouses and collect the receipts as a lump sum payment. The other object of promoting good maintenance standards, however, has also to be kept in view. The sale can take place through a license period of either 30 years or less; it can be stipulated HUDCO can increase the lease money after a stipulated period.

The second option is that the guesthouses can be managed as a company club on membership fee for staying facilities of the officers of various companies. The membership fee could be (a) once in a lifetime charge (b) an annual fee or

(c) a combination of the two. It will be possible to collect higher revenue if the membership is transferable. HUDCO ought to have the authority to increase the uncertainty of a periodic increase in the future, and therefore may prefer (b) The membership fee could be fixed to cover the fixed cost of the project, and charges with utilizing the facilities to cover the variable cost.

It is also possible to auction some Guesthouses, and the rest can be disposed of on a membership basis. Some guesthouses can also be offered to Government organizations, like state government or their institution, on a predetermined premium. The third option is to license the guesthouse on a room night occupancy basis. Each prospective buyer can purchase 150 room nights at a minimum and pay a lump sum amount. After that, the buyer pays only an actual maintenance or housekeeping fee site of the hotel and shopping mall.

It will be best to license out the site of the hotel and shopping mall through an auction. The license will undertake the construction as per urban design. The annual license fee can be increased after a stipulated period. The license will be given the right to sublicense the whole or part of the facilities.

Shopping / Restaurant (Ground floor of Guesthouse): These facilities will be fully developed and licensed out through auction.

Arcade (General Shopping Area): These will be developed and then licensed out through auction for maintaining the integrity of the urban design. The license will provide the license to put up shops of various products.

CULTURAL FACILITIES: The cultural facilities in this block will have to be licensed out on a no-profit, no-loss basis, as per Government policy, that is the actual cost of land and construction. The offices, banks, etc. in the cultural block can be licensed out through auction. It may be appropriate to develop a wing as a business Centre of company liaison offices.

CULTURAL CENTER (AUDITORIUM): There are various ways of handling the disposal. The property owner can be kept with HUDCO and receipts generated through rental on use basic. The other option is to give it to a cultural society and cost amortized through rentals. Still, a third option will be to sell it to a private or government organization for a fixed period of the lease, and the buyer then lets out using the auditorium.

POLYCLINIC: It can be licensed out to various medical specialists at a reserved price. The lease can be for 10 years, but it will be better to give a right of transfer, etc. for predetermined use.
Project cash flows were also discussed, depending upon the option adopted, the following have to be taken into account: 1. Market conditions, 2. Tax treatment of the flow of receipt to HUDCO, 3. The closing cost of the project.

Project receipts-costs were discussed, stating it is difficult to exactly project the receipts from the project. However, the variety of expected receipts can be visualized. These are as follows:

Type of Area	Area (sq. meter)	Date of Completion	Receipt (Rs. In Crores)	
Receipts			Low	High
Offices	5,500	Jan, 1993		
Shopping/Restaurant	11,500	Jan, 1993		
Polyclinic	500	Jan, 1993		
	17,500		48 (@Rs. 27,500 per (US Dollar 1061) Sq. sq. meter	52.50 (@Rs.30,000 US Dollar 1157.40) per Sq. sq. meter
Guesthouse	504 Rooms	Oct., 1991 to Jan., 1992	86 (Rs.7 lakh for 150 nights)	95 (through auction to the Hoteliers)
Hotel Sire		June,1992	32	45
		Total	166	192.50

HUDCO is basically a financing institution and design development and technology promotion organization and has little experience in the disposal of large-scale properties. With this in mind, it is proposed it would be useful to establish a properties' disposal research unit by designing existing officers to perform this role and hire a market and professional for 2-3 months. This property disposal research unit will study the market and propose suitable strategies for disposal. The actual disposal of properties can be handled by land and development offices in the Ministry of Urban Development. It is proposed as L&DO has extensive experience in real estate management.

Is it not a Scam that the Ministry of Urban Development preferred HUDCO to give this project when it was a work of the Central Public Works Department and Delhi Development Authority in the light of admissions by HUDCO?

Chapter: Thirteen

Empowered Committee for Andrews Ganj Was Aware of Unauthorized Constructions by HUDCO at Andrews Ganj

From this Chapter, it is obvious and concluded by me as Author to go deep into the Scam of Andrews Ganj land by HUDCO that the members of the Empowered Committee, which included Government Officers and HUDCO Officers, were well aware that the constructions are going on without any approval of the local bodies, which was violated of various laws of the country. They were also aware that HUDCO is a financing institution and design development and technology promotion organization. They have little experience in the disposal of large-scale properties, and there were Income Tax implications in disposing of the properties by HUDCO being a company incorporated under the Companies Act, 1956. All these aspects were ignored knowingly, leading to a scam.

The Empowered Committee was aware that the disposal of these properties should be handled by the Land & Development office in the Ministry of Urban Development, who had extensive experience in real estate, but everything was ignored intentionally and deliberately.

In the second Empowered Committee held on 19th April 1991 to monitor Andrews Ganj's project named by

HUDCO as HUDCO Place, the description of properties was placed and discussed.

It was finalized that the development will be a Unique Urban Experience consisting of a large plaza for social interaction, cultural center Executive club, basera for low budget tourist hotel, air-conditioned shopping mall polyclinic, restaurants, shop art galleries on the street, open court, and vast landscaped green. These properties will be disposed of in the open market. In the first phase, it is proposed to commission the Guesthouses, with all essential infrastructure being made available by October 1991, when Asian games are likely to be held. In the second phase, it is proposed to complete the construction of an arcade, cultural block, etc. It is proposed to complete phase it by October 1992.

The site for the 12-story hotel and shopping mall can be auctioned at any time, but it will be better to synchronize it with the beginning by phase II. In any case, these plots can be auctioned only after some basic development regarding services has been done.

A complete financial feasibility report needs to be prepared in respect of each element so that the stakes involved in each alternative set of decisions are clear. This shall account for the cost of construction (including interest), overhead costs, any, and the surplus expected if the disposal must be undertaken through HUDCO. The tax implication of it must be taken into account, as advised by our tax consultant (i.e., Sankar Aiyar, a copy of which was circulated to all the members of the Empowered Committee).

It was discussed in the Empowered Committee to monitor Andrews Ganj's project that each element of the property needs not be taken as a profit center, yet one cannot sideline the basic objective of making the project cost-effective and manage the disposal in a manner that maximum surplus is generated for additional pool housing. Options for Disposal were discussed: Guesthouse lumps.

The guesthouses will be managed like a hotel. There are various options to dispose of this property. One option is to auction the Guesthouses and collect the receipts as a lump sum payment. The other object of promoting good maintenance standards, however, has also to be kept in view. The sale can take place through a license period of either 30 years or less; it can be stipulated HUDCO can increase the lease money after a stipulated period.

The second option is that the guesthouses can be managed as a company club on membership fee for staying facilities of the officers of various companies. The membership fee could be (a) once in a lifetime charge (b) an annual fee or (c) a combination of the two. It will be possible to collect higher revenue if the membership is transferable. HUDCO ought to have the authority to increase the uncertainty of a periodic increase in the future, and therefore may prefer (b) The membership fee could be fixed to cover the fixed cost of the project, and charges with utilizing the facilities to cover the variable cost.

It is also possible to auction some Guesthouses, and the rest can be disposed of on a membership basis. Some guesthouses can also be offered to Government organizations, like state government or their institution, on a predetermined premium. The third option is to license the guesthouse on a room night occupancy basis. Each prospective buyer can purchase 150 room nights at a minimum and pay a lump sum amount. After that, the buyer pays only an actual maintenance or housekeeping fee site of the hotel and shopping mall.

It will be best to license out the site of the hotel and shopping mall through an auction. The license will undertake the construction as per urban design. The annual license fee can be increased after a stipulated period. The license will be given the right to sublicense the whole or part of the facilities.

Shopping / Restaurant (Ground floor of Guesthouse): These facilities will be fully developed and licensed out through auction.

Arcade (General Shopping Area): These will be developed and then licensed out through auction for maintaining the integrity of the urban design. The license will provide the license to put up shops of various products.

Cultural Facilities: The cultural facilities in this block will have to be licensed out on a no-profit, no-loss basis, as per Government policy, that is the actual cost of land and construction. The offices, banks, etc. in the cultural block can be licensed out through auction. It may be appropriate to develop a wing as a business Centre of company liaison offices.

Cultural center (Auditorium): There are various ways of handling the disposal. The property owner can be kept with HUDCO and receipts generated through rental on use basic. The other option is to give it to a cultural society and cost amortized through rentals. Still, a third option will be to sell it to a private or government organization for a fixed period of the lease, and the buyer then lets out using the auditorium.

Polyclinic: It can be licensed out to various medical specialists at a reserved price. The lease can be for 10 years, but it will be better to give a right of transfer, etc. for predetermined use.

Project cash flows were also discussed, depending upon the option adopted, the following have to be taken into account: 1. Market conditions, 2. Tax treatment of the flow of receipt to HUDCO, 3. The closing cost of the project.

Project receipts-costs were discussed, stating it is difficult to exactly project the receipts from the project. However, the variety of expected receipts can be visualized. These are as follows:

Type of Area	Area (sq. meter)	Date of Completion	Receipt (Rs. In Crores)	
Receipts			Low	High
Offices	5,500	Jan, 1993		
Shopping/Restaurant	11,500	Jan, 1993		
Polyclinic	500	Jan, 1993		
	17,500		48 (@Rs. 27,500 per (US Dollar 1061)	52.50 (@Rs.30,000 US Dollar 1157.40) per Sq. sq. meter

			Sq. sq. meter	
Guesthouse	504 Rooms	Oct., 1991 to Jan., 1992	86 (Rs.7 lakh for 150 nights)	95 (through auction to the Hoteliers)
Hotel Sire		June,1992	32	45
		Total	166	192.50

HUDCO is basically a financing institution and design development and technology promotion organization and has little experience in the disposal of large-scale properties. With this in mind, it is proposed it would be useful to establish a properties' disposal research unit by designing existing officers to perform this role and hire a market and professional for 2-3 months. This property disposal research unit will study the market and propose suitable strategies for disposal. The actual disposal of properties can be handled by land and development offices in the Ministry of Urban Development. It is proposed as L&DO has extensive experience in real estate management.

Is it not a Scam that the Ministry of Urban Development preferred HUDCO to give this project when it was a work of the Central Public Works Department and Delhi Development Authority in the light of admissions by HUDCO?

Chapter: Fourteen

Empowered Committee Approved the Reserve Prices of The Properties in April 1991

As an author, after going through the scam by HUDCO, it is learned HUDCO was well aware that the land use of Andrews Ganj was restored to Master Plan, 1962, and as per Master Plan 1962, hotel and Guesthouses were not permitted, which was already informed by Municipal Corporation of Delhi to HUDCO and the Ministry. The Empowered Committee members were from the Ministry as well, but they deliberately and intentionally overlooked them. The disposal of the land for a hotel and Guesthouses constructed by HUDCO was planned without any approval of the building layout plans, as well as without the land use.

To place before the second Empowered Committee Meeting, Chairman-cum-Managing Director of HUDCO got framed the disposal policy and cash flow of Andrews Ganj Project on 19th April 1991, which was placed before the Empowered Committee which was approved as follows:

The Ministry of Urban Development has allotted land to HUDCO in Andrews Ganj at a nominal cost of Re.1 and Re.1 as annual ground rent for developing a Community Center on the land, and out of the proceeds realized by disposal of the Community Center, construct General Pool

Accommodation for Central, construct General Pool Accommodation for Central Government Employees on the residential portion of the land. The Community Center land is 17.6 acres and the residential land is 25 acres. In addition, these 18 acres in the same locality have been entrusted to HUDCO without payment of any fee for development and maintenance as a zonal green.

The main consideration of this allotment was that the resources generated through the disposal of the properties should be utilized for the construction of the General Pool Residential Accommodation for Central government employees. Apart from generating such resources and the construction of residential accommodation for government employees without any initial capital investment, the development of the entire area will be based on an integrated urban design form, which will promote various innovative concepts and simultaneously ensure optimum utilization of the land in terms of density of population.

The Community Center will consist of the following categories. Area in sq. sq. meters:

- **Hotel Site 25000**

- **Guesthouse 27500**
- **Shopping Arcade 5500**
- **Shopping Mall 5000**
- **Offices 4000**
- **Cultural center 3000**
- **Community facilities like fire post-1700**

Total 71700

Out of these categories, as per the directions of the Ministry of Urban Development, construction has been started and is in progress in the Guesthouse portion, which is in two clusters of six blocks in each cluster, with a total of 240 rooms. This construction of this portion was taken up, as the Government was keen to have them completed before the Afro-Asian Games.

Decisions of the Committee were taken as required on disposal prices of the properties, mode of disposal, time frame, cost of constructions, the reserve price for hotel land for Rs. 50 crores (US Dollar 21.98 million), Guesthouses fully air-conditioned Rs. 12 lacs per room for 500 rooms, shopping area at Rs. 45000/- (US Dollar 1978) per Sq. Meters. The Committee discussed three alternatives of disposal. Their pros and cons were discussed, all of which were approved.

Is it not a Scam that the Empowered Committee for Andrews Ganj consisting of high-level Officers of the Ministry of Urban Development deliberately and intentionally overlooked the illegal constructions and land use?

Chapter: Fifteen

16th September 1991, Nav Bharat Times, A Newspaper Report Regarding Unauthorized Construction by HUDCO

From the documents, it is clear that any layman could conclude the layout plan was being submitted as per Master Plan, 2001, but the construction was carried out as per Master Plan, 1962, due to which the layout plans were not being approved, but the illegal constructions continued as the target was October 1991 to complete the construction of Guesthouses and other buildings at Andrews Ganj. But the Ministry out of the way informed the Municipal Corporation of Delhi that the plans be sanctioned as per Master Plan- 1962.

Dr. P.S. Rana called 13th for 1991 by September, a meeting, Executive Director, Andrews Ganj project, to discuss the land use of Pinjrapole Andrews Ganj and the approval of a layout plan by Municipal Corporation of Delhi by issuing a letter 9th August 1991 to the Ministry, Delhi Development Authority and other concerned officers. Town Planner, Municipal Corporation of Delhi gave a final reminder on 13th August 1991 to HUDCO for approval of layout plan of Pinjrapole Andrews Ganj project, informing that Delhi Urban Art Commission approval is required for modification as per Master Plan-2001 for which many reminders have been sent. Despite various reminders from time to time, and the meeting held with Additional

Commissioner, Municipal Corporation of Delhi on 21st June 1991, when your architect confirmed that within 15 days the compliance will be made. In pursuance to which the Architect, Mr. Jasbir Sawhney, sought some more time in its letter dated 22nd August 1991.

In the meeting held on 16th August 1991 by Chairman-cum-Managing Director D, HUDCO, Mr. Jasbir Sawhney, Consultant Architect, and Delhi Development Authority, in which it was specifically stated the land use of Community Center at Pinjrapole Andrews Ganj must be changed, which was informed and discussed in members from Ministry, Delhi Development Authority and HUDCO site as well. But it was decided to keep it pending for discussion with the Secretary, Ministry of Urban Development.
On 4th September 1991, the Joint Secretary, Mr. K. Dharmarajan, addressed the letter to HUDCO that about your letter dated 30th August 1991, the Government had decided for development of Pinjrapole area 35 acres, 18 acres, 17 acres as per the Old Master Plan, since at that time when the decision was taken and the proposal approved the new Master Plan had not come into force. You may proceed with the sanction of building plans with

the Municipal Corporation of Delhi, as per old Master Plan provisions. The authorization letter for this purpose.

Simultaneously, Mr. K. Dharmarajan, Joint Secretary, Ministry of Urban Development, on 4th September 1991 issued a letter to whom it may concern:

The government had decided to take up development in the Pinjrapole area, as per the old master plan, providing for 35 acres of housing, 18 acres of zonal green, and 17 acres of Community Center. This decision was taken by the Government before the notification of the Master Plan for Delhi, 2001, and permission was given to Central Public Works Department and HUDCO to develop this area as per the old Master Plan. This is to authorize HUDCO to submit plans to the Municipal Corporation of Delhi for the development of this area, as per provisions in the old Master Plan, 1962.

On 16th September 1991, Nav Bharat Times, a newspaper, published news through a report by Mr. Saurabh Sinha that the Government, through the Ministry of Urban Development and HUDCO, have violated the building laws in South Delhi on 17 acres of land. On this land, they have constructed 4 storied buildings, and it is being tried to regularize buildings. The people in the vicinity of the area have raised objections in respect of these buildings. HUDCO Place near Khelgaon, Andrews Ganj, has constructed the buildings without the sanction of building plans from the Municipal Corporation of Delhi.

Mr. P.K. Khanna, the Building Plans Commissioner, confirmed he has not received any proposal for sanction of the building plan. Delhi Development Authority has stated that as per the Master Plan. HUDCO started the construction in 1990 when it was decided to construct as per the Master Plan for Delhi, 1962. Now HUDCO has constructed the Guesthouses as per the new Master Plan. This land use is to be changed to Pinjrapole. The 17 acres of land have been illegally given to HUDCO. Now Delhi Development Authority has notified New Master Plan, violated by HUDCO by constructing Guesthouses. Now, the difficulty has arisen with the Ministry of Urban Development.

This land spread at the back, being 40 acres had been in a dispute earlier called Pinjrapole. The building constructed has cost HUDCO crores of Rupees. The dispute of the land had arisen earlier than well. All the big business people had been eying this land. The layout plan has been rejected earlier; it was for games, now it is for residential. 17 acres of land have been given for sale. On 25 acres, Government flats have to be made for the Ministry of Urban Development, who has handed over the land to HUDCO, who had started constructions without taking sanction of building plans. There are disputes between the various agencies of this land.

The constructions have been started without any formalities being completed. HUDCO has been constructed in the name of Asian Games in conjunction with the Ministry of Urban Development, while as per the New Master Plan, land use has been changed. But HUDCO has continued the constructions: when the Ministry and HUDCO officials were contacted, they did not want to respond. The people who were constructing were unaware of anything, but they said whatever the Ministry of Urban Development is saying, we are doing it.

The Vice-Chairman, Delhi Development Authority, sought comments on the news to be given within a week, but since the Ministry was involved with HUDCO for the illegal constructions, the query was closed on the news.

The Ministry of Urban Development through Under Secretary Mr. Arjan Dev issued a letter on 24th September 1991 approved by the Joint Secretary Mr. Dharmarajan to Vice Chairman, Delhi Development Authority with a copy of the Secretary, Land & Building Department, Delhi Administration, and the Commissioner, Municipal Corporation of Delhi, Delhi enclosing letter dated 30th August 1991 of Chairman-cum-Managing Director, HUDCO regarding Andrews Ganj project and sought a report in the matter to the Ministry urgently which was acted upon by the office of Vice-Chairman, Delhi Development Authority as well as other departments but as desired the layout plans could have not been approved under the Old Master Plan, 1962 as the land use of Andrews Ganj was for Convention Center and institutional i.e. the land could be allotted only for the development of the institutions and not HUDCO had constructed.

The Chairman cum Managing Director, Mr. S.K. Sharma retired on 30th September 1991, and Mr. PSA Sundaram, Joint Secretary, was given an additional post as Chairman cum Managing Director of HUDCO from 1st October 1991, who remained in HUDCO until 19th March 1992. Mr. V. Suresh was promoted as director (Corporate) on the retirement of Mr. S.K. Sharma, who thereafter continued to control and monitor the Andrews Ganj project. Mr. K. K. Bhatnagar was appointed in March 1992 as Chairman-cum-Managing Director of HUDCO by the Government for 5 years.

It shows to me as an author that the Government was falsely covering HUDCO for the illegal constructions carried out by HUDCO at the behest of the Government. The new Master Plan was notified on 1st August 1990, and the old Master Plan was invalid thereafter unless the plans were approved before 1st August 1990. In the present case, no layout plan was approved, rather not even conceptual approval was given by any of the authorities, because of which letters dated 4th September 1991 and 24th September 1991 were completely illegal, as even the allotment of Andrews Ganj was not issued to Land & Development Officer by the Ministry of Urban Development, which issued on 1st November 1990 after the Master Plan, 2001 was notified.

From here, it is further gathered HUDCO was constructing the buildings before the notification of the Master Plan notified on 1st August 1990, although the formal contracts for construction by HUDCO were given in October 1990, which definitively is a scam with the Ministry of Urban Development and its officers at the relevant time.

The news report was neglected and ignored totally when the Congress Government was in power under the Prime Ministership of Mr. P.V. Narsimha Rao from 21st June 1991, and the Cabinet Minister of Urban Development was Ms. Sheila Kaul and the state minister was Mr. Arunachalam. The New Minister, Ms. Sheila Kaul, shuffled all the officers, including the Secretary, except the Joint Secretary, Mr. K. Dharmarajan. The new Secretary appointed was Mr. R. K Bhargava.

Was it not a scam that illegal constructions reported by the prime newspaper regarding Andrews' Ganj were neglected?

Chapter: Sixteen

Contrary Stands by The Government and HUDCO to the Land Use of Andrews Ganj Land Itself Is A Scam

The scam to maneuver over one Master Plan to another Master Plan for land use of Andrews Ganj is clear from the stands taken by the Government and HUDCO, who were sometimes submitting the plans as per master Plan, 1962, and sometimes as per Master Plan, 2001, taking their stand contrary, which was even noticed by Municipal Corporation of Delhi that the Layout Plan submitted for residence area as per Master Plan, 1962, but the Community Center uses have been of Master Plan, 2001, while the Municipal Corporation of Delhi cannot permit both the master plans in one layout. Now the Government and HUDCO knew well that the amendment in the land use must be notified to get the layout plans approved as per Master Plan, 1962. However, it was noticed as an author that the Government took contrary stands as per their convenience to cover up the scam which had started in 1989-1990 of the Andrews Ganj land. HUDCO, as well as the officers of the Ministry of Urban Development wrongly and falsely submitted to Municipal Corporation of Delhi that the building plans were submitted before Master Plan notification on 1st August 1990, and falsely submitted the layout plans were approved in October 1990 for Andrew Ganj land.

HUDCO's Director (Corporate) Mr. V. Suresh in his letter dated 25th October 1991 informed Mr. GR Ambwani, Engineer in Chief, Municipal Corporation of Delhi regarding the construction of HUDCO Guesthouse Cluster A & B, Andrews Gang–approval of layout plan and building plans referring to letter no. 112871/Bldg./HD2/91/825/682 dated 17th October 1991 issued by Mr. RN Gupta, EE (Bldg.) regarding the construction of HUDCO Guesthouse Cluster A & B, Andrews Gang without the approval of Municipal Corporation of Delhi and the discussion with Mr. P.S.A. Sundaram, J.S. Ministry of Urban Development. I have got the matter examined, and the position is as under:

The layout plan of the above complex was submitted to the town planning department of Municipal Corporation of Delhi, Kashmiri Gate, Delhi on 24th May 1990 based on the 1962 Master Plan.

Simultaneously, a conceptual layout plan was submitted to Delhi Urban Arts Commission in August 1990, which was considered and approved by the Delhi Urban Art Commission in its meeting held on 31st August 1990, as communicated vide the Delhi Urban Art Commission letter of October 1990. Delhi Urban Art Commission. Delhi Urban Art Commission's comments for marginal changes are in respect of the housing area, whereby the seven-story transit hostel block for marginal modifications was advised to submit the revised conceptual layout plan. In any case, work on these transit houses blocks had commenced.

Building plans of the project were given to the Municipal Corporation of Delhi on 31st May 1990, indicating that the layout plan of the project has already been submitted to the Town Planning Department, and it was requested that building plans may be considered for sanction pending approval of the layout plan. It was indicated this is a time-bound Government project for Afro Asian Games to be held in 1991.

One of the main observations of the Town Planning Department, Municipal Corporation of Delhi letter dated 12th February 1991, was that the layout plan should be as per Master Plan, 2001. In this connection, the Government of India had decided to take up the development in the Pinjrapole area as per the old master plan, and the Government took this decision before the notification of the Master Plan for Delhi, 2001. Permission was given to the Central Public Works Department and HUDCO to develop this area as per the old Master Plan. A copy of the letter received from Mr. K. Dharmarajan, Joint Secretary, Ministry of Urban Development, dated 4th September 1991 for ready reference.

It may be mentioned no violation of the Master Plan/building bye-laws has been done. I am informed that the Ministry is also initiating action for change of land use. The work has been started as per instructions of the Government of India, and I have also instructed the Consulting Architects to submit the revised plans, as suggested by your department, which will be submitted by the end of this month to your office, as well as to the Delhi Urban Art Commission.

In view of the above, I hope you will appreciate our difficulty and proceed with the work in the public interest, pending approval of the plans from your department.

Mr. Gopal Krishan Company Secretary HUDCO's letter dated 6th November 1991 to all the members of the monitoring & review committee Regarding the 3rd meeting of the Empowered Committee to review and monitor the project at Andrews Gang to be held on November 12, 1991.

As desired by Additional Secretary, Ministry of Urban Development, the third meeting of the Empowered Committee to review and monitor projects at Andrews Gang will be held on Tuesday, the 12th November 1991 at 10.30 AM at HUDCO House, Lodhi Road, New Delhi - 110003 to discuss disposal policy, cash flow, approval to type design, etc. I am to request you to kindly make it convenient to attend the same.

Mr. Pankaj Agrawala Dy. Secretary (Land) from the Ministry of Urban Development informed on 7th November 1991 to Mr. PP Chauhan Commissioner, Municipal Corporation of Delhi that as you might be aware there is a proposal of Develop in Pinjrapole area (Andrews Ganj) providing for residential housing, 18 acres zonal green, and 17 acres Community Center as per the old master plan. When the development areas were initiated, it was pointed out that in the new master plan; the area had been shown for the convention center and other uses. This Ministry had at that time decided that the development should proceed as per the then prevailing master plan.

Delhi Urban Art Commission has approved the concept plan of HUDCO, except for the transit flats. We have now been informed the Municipal Corporation of Delhi is asking for authorization from our Ministry before considering this proposal. In this connection, I am enclosing a copy of the authorization dated 4th September 1991 from our Ministry to HUDCO to submit plans to the Municipal Corporation of Delhi for the development of this area, as per the provisions of the old master plan. I shall therefore request the plans submitted by HUDCO, as per the provisions of the old Master Plan. Meanwhile, the Delhi Development Authority is being asked to initiate action to restore the land use of the plot as per the 1961 plan.

Mr. P.K. Garg, Regional Chief of HUDCO, on 8th November 1991 submitted a revised layout plan for 35 acres of the site of housing and 17-acre Community Center for approval of Municipal Corporation of Delhi to be considered per old master plan.

Municipal Corporation of Delhi on scrutiny of the proposal for Community Center submitted the layout plan submitted by HUDCO is not following the old master plan, as proposed land use of hotels and Guesthouses are not permitted in the Master Plan 1962. As such, the proposal submitted is not as per the old master plan, also urban usages, etc., and does not qualify for approval and needs to be revised. Moreover, no formal notification changes of land use as per Master Plan for Delhi, 2001 has been received.

Mr. P.K. Garg Regional Chief of HUDCO again requested on 8th November 1991 to the Town Planner Municipal Corporation of Delhi regarding Approval of Layout Plan, Pinjrapole, New Delhi, HUDCO Place Community Center, and Pinjrapole Government Pool Housing, New Delhi. Please refer to your above-cited letter, wherein it was indicated the layout plan submitted required the approval of the Delhi Urban Art Commission/modification as per Master Plan, 2001. In this connection, please find enclosed herewith a copy of letter No. 1817-D/Joint Secretary (Urban Development) dated 4th September 1991, along with an enclosure received from Mr. K Dharmarajan, Joint Secretary (Urban Development), Ministry of Urban Development, and Government of India regarding land use of the Pinjrapole site.

Approval from the Civil Aviation Department, as well as Delhi Electricity Supply Undertaking, is being obtained separately. The Delhi Urban Arts Commission has already cleared the conceptual plans to vide their letter dated 19th October 1990. Our architect has also revised the layout plan/drawings, keeping in view the Municipal Corporation of Delhi's earlier observations. Four copies of the layout plan duly signed by the architect and the owner. This decision was taken by the Government before the Notification of the Master Plan for Delhi 2001 on 1st August 1990, and permission was given to the Central Public Works Department and HUDCO for development for this area per the old Master Plan.

It is seen by me as an author that they were a contrary stand of the Government and HUDCO in respect to the land use of Andrews Ganj land. As per the letter of the Government, it shows that the Government had decided to take up development in the Pinjrapole area, as per the old master plan providing for 35 acres of housing, is acres of zonal green, and 17 acres of Community Center. It is observed the land-use change was required, and the layout plans submitted for Community Center were as per the Master Plan, 2001, but on the other side, one-person Joint Secretary Mr. K. Dharmarajan insisted the construction by HUDCO be permitted as per the old Master Plan, 1962.

The Scam…. was is not done by the Government and HUDCO to maneuver over one Master Plan to another for land use of Andrews Ganj? It was observed by the Municipal Corporation of Delhi that the Layout Plan submitted for residence area is as per Master Plan, 1962, but the Community Center uses have been of Master Plan, 2001?

Chapter: Seventeen

Land Use for Building Hotel at Andrews Ganj Not Permitted as Per Master Plan 1962, but Empowered Committee Did Not Bother

On reading the observations, my view as an author is that the Municipal Corporation of Delhi, who had observed in writing on the layout plans submitted by HUDCO, concluded by me that usage under Community Center as per Master Plan, 1962 are to be followed, but on the contrary, usage for Community Center has been taken of Master Plan, 2001 and land use as per Master Plan, 1962. It was categorically decided that as per the old Master Plan, the Community Center does not include hotels and Guesthouses which cannot be approved as per the old Master Plan, 1962. The layout plan needed revision as per Master Plan for Delhi, 1962, since Joint Secretary of the Ministry of Urban Development had stated Master Plan, 1962 would be applicable, and the current land use of Master Plan, 2001 of Andrews Ganj is being notified for change in land use of Andrews Ganj to be restored to Master Plan, 1962.

But HUDCO, despite the problem in land use, continued to discuss in the Empowered Committee meetings that the disposal of hotel sites after the land-use change, as per the Master Plan for Delhi, 1962, should be taken up at first instance, and the disposal of guest house blocks. HUDCO did not bother whether a hotel or guest houses would be permitted or not. HUDCO continued to violate all the laws of the Country for Delhi Administration in the disposal of these properties.

Municipal Corporation of Delhi placed the note on 19th November 1991 before the Committee referring to a letter from Mr. P.K. Garg, HUDCO, and Mr. V. Suresh dated 8th November 1991 and 25th October 1991, enclosing a letter from Joint Secretary, Ministry of Urban Development letter dated 4th September 1991. Those building plans were to be considered per the provision of the old master plan, 1962. As such, this scrutinizing FAR, density for residential Performa and usage under Community Center as per Master Plan, 1962 are to be followed, but on the contrary, usage for Community Center has been taken of Master Plan, 2001 and land use as per Master Plan, 1962.
As per Master Plan, 1962 for the Community Center allowed many shops 80-100, RBS, Cinema, Petrol Pump, Shopping and Service industries, post office, telephone office, telephone exchange, police station, fire station, health care. However, the proposal for Community Center includes hotels, guesthouses, etc., is not permissible as per the Master Plan for Delhi 1962, and the proposal needs revision as per the Master Plan for Delhi, 1962. The letter

is issued provided formal notification considering this Master Plan Delhi, 1962, was revised.

In pursuance of the notice from the Municipal Corporation of Delhi, HUDCO conveyed a meeting on 13th September 1991 at 2.30 pm at HUDCO house, where members of Delhi Development Authority, Urban Ministry, and Architect were present to discuss the approval of the layout plan in the meeting. Delhi Development Authority member pointed out that the land use of the site proposed for a Community Center and staff housing at Sports Authority of India is earmarked for institutional use, and so further approval as such could not be permitted.

Accordingly, the matter was taken up by HUDCO with the Ministry and Delhi Development Authority and Director Corporate Planning, the letter from Joint Secretary, Ministry of Urban Development conveying that the Government had decided for providing 35 acres for housing before Master Plan for Delhi, 2001 accordingly permission was given to Central Public Works Department and HUDCO for development of spite and approval of plans from Municipal Corporation of Delhi. Further, Joint Secretary also stated HUDCO should submit plans to

Municipal Corporation of Delhi as per permissible of Master Plan 1962, and separate action is being taken for notifying the changes of land uses.

The 3rd meeting of the Empowered Monitoring & Review Committee of Andrews Ganj was held on 13th November 1991 in the Conference Room of Additional Secretary, Ministry of Urban Development, Nirman Bhawan, New Delhi in which Mr. RV Pillai-Additional Secretary Ministry of Urban Development (in the chair), Mr. PSA Sundram–Chairman-cum-Managing Director, HUDCO, Mr. Dharmarajan–Joint Secretary (Lands), Mr. B. Bhattacharya–Joint Secretary (Finance), Mr. V. Suresh–Director, HUDCO, Mr. Gopal Krishan–Company Secretary, HUDCO in which disposal Policy and cash flow Andrews Gang were discussed.

It was decided that for Hotel Site, action may be initiated to dispose of the hotel site in the first instance after the Delhi Development Authority approves the land-use change. The procedure for auctioning this plot may be broad on the lines adopted by the Ministry for auction of Windsor Place Hotel site. Regarding the mode of disposal, it was decided the site may be disposed of on a leasehold basis by charging a one-time premium and annual ground rent. The reserve price for the auction may be fixed after conducting a market survey to ascertain the likely return. The time frame for disposal was fixed by the Committee, i.e., for immediate disposal.

Is it not a scam that the current land use of Master Plan, 2001 of Andrews Ganj restored to Master Plan, 1962, but Community Center was constructed and being sold as per Master Plan, 2001?

Chapter: Eighteen

Hotel Earmarked in The Community Center at Andrews Ganj Although as Per Master Plan 1962 Not Permitted

From the ongoing documents referred to by me in my possession, it is observed by me that the objections of ongoing constructions were objected to by the Municipal Corporation of Delhi, but HUDCO went ahead constructing the buildings and continued under Mr. V. Suresh, the action plan for disposal of the hotel site and guesthouse blocks. It was already decided that land-use change was required and that the land use would be as per the Master Plan, 1962. HUDCO still earmarked the hotel plot on the site, which was not allowed in the Master Plan 1962, as per the Municipal Corporation of Delhi and Delhi Development Authority. HUDCO bi passed all the authorities under the umbrella of the Ministry of Urban Development.

As per me, based on the documents, even the Empowered Committee illegally approved the action plan, and the anticipated surplus and cash flow were also planned without any proper land use of the Andrews Ganj land. HUDCO has also appointed a private consultant who had made a presentation to the Secretary, Ministry of Urban Development in September 1991, only on concept urban design. In this meeting, the constraint of land use was considered, but ignored deliberately and intentionally, which let HUDCO go on with the constructions.

The Joint Secretary (Land) Mr. K. Dharmarajan of the Ministry of Urban Development, who was in total control of the Andrews Ganj, decided that as per the Master Plan for Delhi 2001, the detailed urban form study is a prerequisite condition for any development proposed in the Lutyens Delhi to formulate specific norms for accentuating the existing charter.

In spite of the rejection by Municipal Corporation of Delhi of the layout plans of Andrews Ganj, Mr. P.K. Garg, Regional Chief, HUDCO through a letter dated 23rd November 1991 to the Town Planner, Municipal Corporation of Delhi insisted regarding approval of the layout plan, Pinjrapole, New Delhi, referring to letter no. 1/25/90/TP/9439/92 of 13th August 1991 of Municipal Corporation of Delhi, and in continuation of HUDCO's letter dated 8th November 1991 forwarded the revised layout plans without considering the land use of hotel and Guesthouses not permitted in law.

HUDCO decided in the board meeting item no. 4.2.1, the follow-up action on the decisions of the Government Monitoring and Review Committee. Consequently, upon the decisions of the Committee in the last meeting, the following will be an action plan in respect of the disposal of the Hotel site and Guesthouses, and for setting up a Society for Estate Management.

Action Plan for disposal of Hotel Site was decided to expedite Delhi Development Authority's decision on land-use change. Earmark hotel plot on the site by parameters and bounds, and prepare a sketch. Fix the reserve price and installments concerning the plan for general pool construction during the next financial year, finalize terms of disposal and stipulation, etc. Advertise for applications for shortlisting. Process application and prepare a shortlist. Fix a time for the auction.

Guesthouses it was decided to work out costs more accurately concerning area, market position, etc. Fix the price for disposal and timing for disposal concerning the plan for General Pool Construction next year. Write to State Governments and Public Sector Undertakings calling for options. Screen the requests and prepare the list for disposal. The Committee had approved the action plan.

The Joint Secretary of the Ministry of Urban Development, Mr. K. Dharmarajan, confirmed on 4th December 1991 to Mr. Joglekar, Executive Director, HUDCO that in so far as debiting that cost of the studies to the Andrews Ganj Project is concerned, while the government is agreeable to it in principle, we would like to have information regarding the cost of the various studies, so that the government can give a formal clearance in this regard in consultation with the integrated finance.

The Ministry of Urban Development vide its letter dated 31st October 1991, entrusted to HUDCO to conduct the urban design study to accommodate general pool housing (spillover of Andrews Ganj Project) of higher-order and transit hostels in three pockets of land measuring around 13 acres in this complex.

As per Master Plan for Delhi 2001, the detailed urban form study is a prerequisite condition for any development proposed in the Lutyens Delhi to formulate specific norms for accentuating the existing charter.

Latest Status: A presentation was made in Secretary, Ministry of Urban Development on 11th September 1991 of the conceptual urban design for the total study area of about 71 hectares of land. The comprehensive study contained the detailed analysis of existing constraints and potentials in terms of land use, physical environment, density/ground coverage, and the proposal in terms of norms/standards for built-form, landscape, circulation, phasing of development, and a specific proposal for three pockets.

With certain reservations, by and large, the proposal was appreciated, and it was suggested this could be taken into consideration by agencies like Delhi Development Authority in finalizing the Zonal Plan of Pataudi House Areas.

The Ministry of Urban Development has yet to accord its approval for the conceptual design of three pockets. However, the Ministry of Urban Development in its letter dated 4th December 1991 has instructed us to hold on to the study until the parameters for the Lutyens bungalow zone are finalized, which is being settled separately.

The Ministry of Urban Development on 4th December 1991 requested HUDCO keep the study in abeyance until the parameters for development in Lutyens Delhi are framed.

A letter was sent to the architect consultant to stop further work. As per the letter of the Ministry of Urban Development, HUDCO sent a letter to the consultant to hold back the study.

Isn't it a scandal that such huge constructions at Andrews Ganj by HUDCO without sanctions of building plans were allowed by the Municipal Corporation of Delhi to go on without objecting?

Chapter: Nineteen

Empowered Committee of Andrews Ganj Proposed to Be Abolished

In the present scenario, in 1991, it is seen by me that Mr. V. Suresh, Corporate Planning Director, controlled the entire Andrews Ganj project, including the disposal policy, as well as the valuations of the properties and the costs to be incurred by HUDCO. He cleverly changed the name of the Empowered Committee for monitoring the Andrews Ganj project to his own director's Monitoring Committee for the Andrews Ganj project. Thus, after the 4th meeting, there was no Empowered Committee for the Andrews Ganj project, despite the terms of allotment letter issued by the Government of India to the Land & Development Officer of the Andrews Ganj land.

Mr. V. Suresh even placed the new revised calculations and cash flow statements in the 4th meeting before demolishing the Empowered Committee. He also approved 17% interest to be charged on the investments on the Andrews Ganj project.

The Empowered Committee for Andrews Ganj project monitoring the project held the 4th meeting on 2nd December 1991, wherein the committee discussed the nomenclature of the committee, as indicated in the ministry's allotment letter dated 1st November 1990 to the Land & Development Officer, under which the committee was set up. It was desired it should be clarified that this committee would have the status of an empowered committee, only for decisions to be taken by the Ministry of Urban Development, and so far as HUDCO related matters are concerned, the committee will be known as a review & monitoring committee.

When the decision of the committee was taken in the 4th meeting held on 2nd December 1991 was placed before the HUDCO's committee of directors for formal ratification, the committee of directors decided to defer the matter until the Ministry of Urban Development issues the clarification as sought for. Clarification regarding the status of the committee was sought by HUDCO from the Ministry of Urban Development.

The committee approved in their 4th meeting, held on 2nd December 1991, the revised calculation of anticipated surplus and cash flow statements following the disposal policy earlier approved by the committee. The disposal policy as approved by the committee, together with the above statements, was forwarded formally to the Ministry of Urban Development in HUDCO's communication on dated 7th January 1992, informing that the communication dated 31st July 1991 shall stand revised only to the extent of construction costs, anticipated revenue out of the disposals of properties following the disposal policy, and cash flow of our communication dated 7th January 1992.

Before arriving at the funds which would be available for the construction of the general pool accommodation for the Government by HUDCO, the financial charges shown as items 3,4 & 5 of the communication dated 31st July 1992 shall be taken into account. These items are regarding HUDCO overheads, escalation charges & interest on HUDCO investments.

While the figures indicated in the said communication may be taken tentatively, it is clarified HUDCO's charge will be 1.5 percent respectively till the construction is completed, while interest charges at 17 percent on cash outflow shall be until there is outgo of funds from HUDCO's resources and till funds inflow are generated out of the disposal of the various properties as per the disposal policy.

Mr. Gopal Krishan, Company Secretary, HUDCO through a letter dated 30th December 1991 sent to all the members of the Monitoring & Review Committee minutes of a 4th meeting of the Monitoring & Review Committee held on

2nd December 1991 in the Chamber of Mr. RV Pillai, Additional Secretary, Ministry of Urban Development.

I have the honor to forward herewith the minutes of the 4th meeting of the Monitoring & Review Committee held on 2nd December 1991 in the Chamber of Mr. RV Pillai, Additional Secretary, Ministry of Urban Development, Nirman Bhawan, New Delhi.

The Committee observed that the nomenclature of the Committee is "Monitoring and Review Committee" and not the "Empowered Committee". The Director (Corporate Planning) HUDCO clarified the misunderstanding in the name of the committee has arisen due to the language used in the Ministry's order constituting the Committee. It was desired it should be clarified that this Committee would have the status of Empowered Committee only for the decision taken by the Ministry of Urban Development, and so far as HUDCO related matters are concerned, the Committee will be known as Review and Monitoring Committee.

At the outset, Mr. MN Joglekar, Executive Director (Design & Development) HUDCO informed the Committee that he had gone through the minutes of the 3rd meeting of the monitoring & review committee held on 13th November 1991, and the conceptual designs presented by the architects to the Committee. The Committee was informed he will examine the designs in detail, and a detailed report will be submitted to the Committee in the next meeting.

The Committee noted the action plan to expedite land-use change. The Committee was of the view that as the Delhi Development Authority's Technical Committee followed the usual procedure in such cases is lengthy and will delay the matter, the Government will consider directions to the Delhi Development Authority in this regard under the Delhi Development. Act.

Keeping in mind the experience of Delhi Development Authority and the difficulties experienced by them in recuperating installments from prospective buyers, and the fact that cash flow is an important factor here to enable HUDCO to carry out General Pool construction. The Committee decided that the hotel site may be sold outright by recuperation of the entire price in one lump sum, instead of offering to recover the same in installments.

The Committee also decided HUDCO may make a reference to the Income-Tax Authorities, explaining the case and bringing out the fact that HUDCO is only acting as an agent of the Government, and will be utilizing the proceeds by the sale of these properties only for construction of General Pool accommodation for the Government, and that the surplus does not constitute a profit for the Company. Exemption under the Income Tax Act from payment of Income Tax on the surplus proceeds may be sought from the Income-Tax Authorities under the provisions of the Income Tax Act, 1961.

The Committee noted the revised calculation of anticipated surplus and cash flow and decided that the same be forwarded to the Ministry of Urban Development by HUDCO for information. The Chairman desired that for each item, the criteria for arriving at Return may be indicated. It was decided a column may be added to the statement. Accordingly:

	Category	Returns anticipated in crores of Rupees	Criteria for arriving at anticipated Returns
1	**Hotel Site**	50.00 (US Dollar 21.98 million)	The anticipated return is Rs. 50 crores (US Dollar 21.98 million) which will be the reserve price for auction. This price has been fixed on the basis of the notified commercial rate (reduced to 100 FAR) + 20% + the proportionate cost of construction for the common facilities to be utilized by the hotel.
2	**Guesthouse**	50.00 (US Dollar 21.98 million)	The disposal price anticipated is Rs. 58 crores (US Dollar 25.50 million) which is calculated at Rs. 12 lakhs per room for 480 rooms. The cost is based on proportionate land cost on the basis of notified commercial rate + 20% cost of construction and proportionate cost of common facilities.

3	**Shops in Guesthouse, Arcade & Mall**	58.00 (US Dollar 25.50 million)	The total returns anticipated out of the shops in the above categories have been estimated at Rs. 58 crores (US Dollar 25.50 million). This is on the basis of Rs. 45000/- (US Dollar 1978) per sq. Sq. meter Considering the locational advantage and facilities provided and comparing the same with the price fetched in shops constructed by NBCC and disposed of in Bhikaji Cama Place.
4	Offices	10.00	The anticipated return is Rs. 10 crores, which is at the rate of Rs. 275000/- per sq. Meter. This is based on the price fetched by NBCC in Bhikaji Cama Place.
5	Cultural Centre Plot	3.50	Anticipated return is Rs. 3.50 crores (US Dollar 1.53 million) which is at the rate of Rs. 10500/- (US Dollar 461.74) per sq. Meter. As there are no notified rates for disposal of Cultural Centre to private organizations through sale, a suitably lower rate than

			the notified commercial rate has been adopted.

The entire exercise of disposal policy was against the land use for the hotel but HUDCO very cleverly through Mr. V Suresh continued to take their own decisions which led to the scam of the Andrews Ganj project. Isn't this a scandal?

Chapter: Twenty

Government Admitted HUDCO Constructed Without Approvals from Local Bodies

From the entire records of the Ministry, it reveals to me that the change of land use to Master Plan was approved by the Ministry of Urban Development to restore the land use retrospectively to Master Plan for Delhi, 1962, and to do the needful it was sent to Delhi Development Authority, being the agency for change of land use. The Government also made a note in the files that HUDCO had started constructions without approvals, as per Government directions for constructing Guesthouses and car parks. Thus, the Government knew well the Guesthouses were unauthorized.

For the parking objections by the Municipal Corporation of Delhi, the Government stated they are not in favor of recommending and relaxing, so far as Master Plan and Bye-laws requirements are to be complied with. But the Government did not bother about the major construction of Guesthouses and car parks already constructed by HUDCO, which was illegal and against the Master Plan as well as bye-laws.

It is established from the documents that HUDCO and Government both knew that the land use being restored retrospectively to Master Plan 1962 would not permit the construction of hotels and Guesthouses, but still, the disposal plans continued by HUDCO and Government, knowing fully well the violations being committed leading to another Andrews Ganj scam[1].

The land-use changes of Andrews Ganj were proposed on 10th December 1991 by the Deputy Secretary of the Ministry that the Ministry of Urban Development desires detailed information regarding the location and area of land in Andrews Ganj allotted to HUDCO. They required this information for processing the case of a change of land use. The details have been collected from records available with us, and a site plan has been prepared.

There were two alternatives, one for inviting objections/suggestions from the public under Rule 11 A of the Delhi Development Act, and another for issuing a direction to Delhi Development Authority by the Central Government under section 41 of the Act.

The most important issue arising was that the long way to earlier land use retrospectively, alternatively, it can affect only prospectively as the acts specifically lay down such

---

[1] (Azar, 2021)

provision. In the latter case, a prospective legit money compounding fee penalty may be leviable by Municipal Corporation of Delhi by the work already started, as per Government directions of constructing Guesthouses, car parks, and type-VI flats, unless the compounding fee is waived off.

The proposal was discussed with the Joint Secretary by the Under Secretary and the Director of the Ministry of Urban Development, which was put up by the consultant, Mr. N. Rajagopalan of the Ministry of Urban Development, submitted on 12th December 1991 to Mr. Pankaj Aggarwal, Deputy Secretary of the Ministry of Urban Development. Mr. Pankaj Aggarwal was directed to take the necessary action as per alternative-2. It was further approved on 29th December 1991 by Joint Secretary, Additional Secretary, as discussed with the Minister on 26th December 1991, deciding to issue a direction to Delhi Development Authority under Section 41 of the Delhi Development Act. The decision was communicated to HUDCO on 30th December 1991.

HUDCO recorded in its Directors Committee Meeting in December 1991 that the land-use problem of Andrews Ganj project land has been finally sorted out by the Ministry of Urban Development, who have obtained the approval of the Urban Development Minister to issue direction to Delhi Development Authority under section 41 of the Delhi Development Act that the land use shall be as was existing in the 1962 master plan. The ministry will shortly issue the notification. The Municipal Corporation of Delhi, to whom the consulting architect submitted the plan M/s Jasbir Sawhney Associated, made certain observations that had a significant impact on the layout plan.

It was clarified the Government is not in favor of recommending any relaxation, so far as the master plan and Bylaw's requirement complies.

The Town Planner, Municipal Corporation of Delhi, Mr. A.P. Sethi, on 31st December 1991, in respect of a meeting held on 20th December 1991, informed M/s. Jasbir Sawhney & Associates regarding revised layout plan for General Pool Housing and Community Center for sports authority of India at Pinjrapole, New Delhi, that the above-mentioned layout plan was considered by Additional Commissioner in the meeting held on 20th December 1991, and was rejected for resubmission with the observations.

The Architect/applicant furnished the subsequent Delhi Development Authority decision. The clearance of Delhi Electricity Supply Undertaking in respect of electric sub-station be furnished by the applicant. The copy of Item No. 344/91 considered by Municipal Corporation of Delhi in respect of Layout Plan for General Pool Housing Community Center for Sports Authority of India at Pinjrapole, New Delhi was attached for resubmission.

Chapter: Twenty-One

Restoration of Land Use of Andrews Ganj To Be Restored to Master Plan 1962 Did Not Permit the Community Center to Have Hotel and Guesthouses

On resubmission of the layout plan by HUDCO, the observations were made by the Municipal Corporation of Delhi[2]. The Central Public Works Department earlier submitted the above-mentioned proposal for Community Center and residential use on a total site measuring 71.20 acres, as per provisions of MP 1962. However, a small pocket, comprising 256 units on part of this site, was earlier approved by Standing Committee vide resolution no. 713/standing dated 21st January 1991, after the same was approved by Delhi Urban Art Commission.

During the pendency of this proposal, the Master Plan for Delhi 2001 was enforced with effect from 1st August 1990, and the applicant was asked to modify the proposal as per provisions of MP 2001, as the land use of this site was changed to social institutions.

A meeting was convened by HUDCO, who was entrusted with the design and development of the site through their Architect on 13th September 1991, to discuss the problem arising out of land use of this site as/MP 2001, and it transpired in the meeting that matter be taken up with Delhi

[2] (Municipal Corporation of Delhi, n.d.)

Development Authority by HUDCO[3] and Ministry of Urban Development for carrying out the proposal as per the old Master Plan, as the scheme was submitted before 1st August 1990.

Now Joint Secretary, Ministry of Urban Development vide letter dated 4th September 1991 addressed to Chairman HUDCO, has stated the decision of implementation of this scheme was taken up by the Ministry at the time of the old Master Plan and New Master Plan, and not come into force at that time. The case may be processed accordingly, as per the provision of the old Master Plan, and further stated that separate action is being taken for notifying the change of land use.

Accordingly, their Architects have submitted the revised Layout Plan for approval, as per the old Master Plan i.e., M.P. 1962. On scrutiny of the scheme following observations have been made:

[3] (Housing and Urban Development Corporation Ltd., n.d.)

Sl	Category	Area in Sq.M.	Cost of Construction Rs. In crores
1	Hotel Site	25,000	11.88 (US Dollar 5.22 million)
2	Guesthouses	25,000	41.85 (US Dollar 18.40 million)
3	Shops in Guesthouses	2500	
4	Shops in Arcade	5,500	8.95 (US Dollar 3.93 million)
5	Shops in mall	5,500	8.05 (US Dollar 3.54 million)
6	Offices	4,000	6.40 (US Dollar 2.81 million)
7	Zonal Green and Horticulture	-	2.09 (US Dollar 0.91 million)
		Total	79.22 (US Dollar 34.83 million)
	Category	Returns anticipated in crores of Rupees	Criteria for arriving at anticipated Returns

1	Hotel Site	50.00 (US Dollar 21.98 million)	The anticipated return is Rs. 50 crores (US Dollar 21.98 million) which will be the reserve price for auction. This price has been fixed on the basis of the notified commercial rate (reduced to 100 FAR) + 20% + the proportionate cost of construction for the common facilities to be utilized by the hotel.
2	Guesthouse	50.00 (US Dollar 21.98 million)	The disposal price anticipated is Rs. 58 crores (US Dollar 25.50 million) which is calculated at Rs. 12 lakhs per room for 480 rooms. The cost is based on proportionate land cost on the basis of notified commercial rate + 20% cost of construction and proportionate cost of common facilities.
3	Shops in Guesthouse, Arcade & Mall	58.00 (US Dollar 25.50 million)	The total returns anticipated out of the shops in the above categories have been estimated at Rs. 58 crores (US Dollar 25.50 million). This is on the basis of Rs. 45000/- (US Dollar 1978) per sq. Sq. meter Considering the locational advantage and facilities provided and comparing

			the same with the price fetched in shops constructed by NBCC and disposed of in Bhikaji Cama Place.
4	Offices	10.00	The anticipated return is Rs. 10 crores, which is at the rate of Rs. 275000/- per sq. Meter. This is based on the price fetched by NBCC in Bhikaji Cama Place.
5	Cultural Centre Plot	3.50	Anticipated return is Rs. 3.50 crores (US Dollar 1.53 million) which is at the rate of Rs. 10500/- (US Dollar 461.74) per sq. Meter. As there are no notified rates for disposal of Cultural Centre to private organisations through sale, a suitably lower rate than the notified commercial rate has been adopted.

In view of the above, the layout plan submitted as per Master Plan for Delhi, 1962 would be considered after the land-use change notification to Master Plan for Delhi, 1962, and the uses of Community Center as per Master Plan, 1962 be modified in the layout plan, and the same be resubmitted since hotel and Guesthouses are not allowed in the Master Plan, 1962, and the layout plan of Andrews Ganj 71 acres cannot be considered partly under 1962 Master Plan and partly under Master Plan, 2001.

Municipal Corporation of Delhi issued the letter to HUDCO and Ministry of Urban Development on 4th January 1992, after approval of the Higher Authorities, all the observations that hotel and Guesthouses are not permitted in Master Plan, 1962, and the residential is not permitted in Master Plan, 2001, given which the revised layout plans be submitted for consideration as per Master Plan for Delhi, 1962 since the Ministry of Urban Development has submitted the land use is being restored of Andrews Ganj.

Mr. Pankaj Aggarwal, Deputy Secretary, Ministry of Urban Development, on 6th January 1992 contacted Municipal Corporation of Delhi, obtaining the noting from Municipal

Corporation of Delhi as desired by Joint Secretary, Urban Development, and collected from Land & Development Office a list of all Government lands in Delhi where Delhi Development Authority has changed the land use in the revised Master Plan from residential to other uses.
He informed Municipal Corporation of Delhi that the Ministry is proposing to issue a direction to Delhi Development Authority under section 41 of the DD Act that the land use of all these lands will revert to Master Plan use of 1962 plan on the ground that General Pool Accommodation should have priority. These lands include Andrews Gang. The direction is expected to be issued by the following date.

Further, on 15th January 1992, the Municipal Corporation of Delhi made the note it is understood from the Ministry that the proposal to issue a direction under section 41 of the Delhi Development Authority Act has been cleared by Secretary, Urban Development, and submitted to Urban Development Minister for approval.

It was definite now that Minister of Urban Development, Mrs. Sheila Kaul, the Minister under the Prime Ministership of Mr. Narasimha Rao, the change of land use of Andrews Ganj land by restoring it retrospectively to Master Plan 1962, was approved. This land-use of Andrews Ganj was changed to get the residential buildings for Government, but the uses of the Community Center as per the Master Plan 1962 did not permit the use for hotel and Guesthouses.

Isn't it a scam that to regularize residential constructions, the land use of Andrews Ganj was restored to Master Plan 1962, without bothering with the land use of the Community Center as the plan was to cheat the prospective investor?

Chapter: Twenty-Two

HUDCO To Get 29.5% Off the Andrews Ganj Project and 17% Interest on The Investments

As an author and as a normal public, my observations are that from the details submitted by HUDCO, it seems HUDCO intended to get about 29.5% with an additional 17% interest on the amounts put in for construction costs. This made HUDCO get more than Rs 35 crores besides interest.

By October 1991, the constructions by HUDCO of the Guesthouse Blocks at Andrews Ganj were complete without any approval of any layout plan, building plan, etc. HUDCO's director (Corporate Planning), Mr. V Suresh submitted to Mr. K. Dharmarajan Joint Secretary Ministry of Urban Development on 7th January 1992 referring to a letter dated 31st July 1991 seeking approval of the government for Andrews Ganj Project. Mr. V. Suresh forwarded the disposal policy of Andrews Ganj properties as approved by the government monitoring and review committee, statements indicating the estimated cost of contraction, anticipated surplus, and anticipated cash flow approved by the said committee. He submitted:

The disposal policy of Andrews Ganj properties, as approved by the Government Monitoring and Review Committee for the hotel site, was to be disposed of by auction after land use of the site is regularized. The mode of disposal shall be by lease. Guesthouses were agreed to be disposed of when ready.

ANDREWS GANJ PROJECT ESTIMATED COST OF CONSTRUCTION

S. No	Category	Returns anticipated (Rs in crores)	Basis of calculation of returns
1	Hotel Site	50.00 (US Dollar 21.98 million)	Reserve Price fixed on the basis of notified commercial rare up to 31st March 1991 +20% + proportionate cost of construction of common facilities.
2	Guesthouses	58.00 (US Dollar 25.50 million)	Land cost on the basis of notified rate up to 31st March 1991 + 20% cost of construction + proportionate cost of common facilities.

3	shops	58.00 (US Dollar 25.50 million)	On the basis of Rs 45000/- (US Dollar 1978.89) per sq. meter considering the locational advantage and facilities provided and comparing with price fetched in shops sold by NBCC at Bhikaji Cama Place.
4	offices	10.00 (US Dollar 4.39 million)	Rs. 27,500 (US Dollar 1209.32) per sq. meter based on the price fetched by NBCC at Bhikaji Cama Place.
5	Cultural Centre	3.50 (US Dollar 1.53 million)	Rs. 10,500 (US Dollar 461.74) per sq. meter Notified commercial rate suitably reduced.
	Total	179.50 (US Dollar 78.93 million)	

Anticipated cost of Construction Rs.79.50 Crores (US Dollar 34.96 million) Net returns anticipated Rs.100.00 Crores (US Dollar 43.97 million)

TENTATIVE PROJECT COSTING

- 3% contingencies 200.23 lacs
- Administration Charges @ 10%, including fee for architects, project management, Chartered Accountants and NIDC. 667.43 lacs
- Overhead of HUDCO, including management time @ 1.5% 100.00 Escalation on Rs 7541.92 crores (US Dollar 33.16 million) @ 15% for project period 1,131.29 lacs
- Interest @ 17% as per norms for financing such projects
- For one year on total outgo, i.e., on Rs. 8673.21 lacs. 1,474.45 lacs Total Rs. 3,573.40 lacs

HUDCO was illegally developing the project at Andrews Ganj, since they were only interested in their margin of 29.5%, with 17% interest in financing the project and making money in the materials, as they were not being purchased at Central Public Works Department fixed rates.

Isn't it a scam that the Government-owned company, HUDCO, was charging 17% interest with compounded interest quarterly on their investment in the Andrews Ganj project, despite their margin of 29% and a lot under the table as well?

Chapter: Twenty-Three

Hotel Still Planned as Per MPD 2001

It is a matter of record seen by me to write this book on HUDCO Scam that although Municipal Corporation of Delhi had informed the Government and HUDCO that as per Master Plan 1962, the guesthouse and hotel are not permitted in the Community Center, still the Committee for Andrews Ganj Project continued to go-ahead for a 5-Star hotel in the Community Center, and in any case, the guest houses were already completed in 1991, which were illegal.

The Company Secretary of HUDCO, Mr. Gopal Krishan, informed on 5th February 1992 to all the members of the Monitoring & Review Committee Regarding the 5th meeting of the Monitoring & Review Committee on Andrews Ganj to be held on Monday, February 10, 1992, and on 10th February, the minutes were recorded of the meeting in which the present members were Mr. RV Pillai-: Additional Secretary Ministry of Urban Development (in Chair), Dr. Sundaram- Chairman & Managing Director. HUDCO, Mr. K Dharamarajan- Joint Secretary (Lands), Ministry of Urban Development, Mr. B Bhattacharya- Joint Secretary (Finance), Ministry of Urban Development, Mr. V Suresh - Director (Corporate Planning), HUDCO, Mr. MN Joglekar - Executive Director (Design Development), Mr. Gopal Krishan - Company Secretary, HUDCO.

The committee noted the hotel can form a part of the Community Center, as per the master plan provisions. Regarding the height of the building, the committee noted as, against the proposal of 36 meters, the Community Center building could provide a maximum of 26 meters height, as per MP 2001. In this connection, the committee also noted an exclusive hotel building can have a height of up to 50 meters, and the fact that the total height for the hotel can be provided within a district center beyond 37 meters. The committee decided that the matter may be discussed with the Delhi Development Authority/Municipal Corporation of Delhi, and the need for retaining the proposed height of 36 meters for the hotel may be impressed upon them. If any further decision of the committee is required after the discussions, the matter may be brought before the committee.

The committee also decided there is a need for a review of parking norms for residential spaces via-a-via office space, as provided for in MP 2001, and the government could take this up with Delhi Development Authority for changes on a realistic footing.

To effectively consume the surplus funds generated from the commercial component of the Andrews Ganj Project, and to accommodate spillover of general pool housing on other available lands, these projects have been identified by the Ministry of Urban Development. While transferring the land required for the Andrews Ganj project, the Ministry of Urban Development has directed HUDCO to maintain a separate account of come and expenditure. Therefore, this issue was brought to the notice of the HUDCO Board in its 149th meeting held on 31st December 1991; the expenses incurred on these studies to be debited to the separate account maintained for Andrews Ganj Project.

Delhi Urban Art Commission in its 694th meeting held on 13th March 1992 did not approve the concept submitted of Andrews Ganj land, and the architect was advised to submit the revised sketches for early consideration of the commission.

Mr. R.K. Bhargava, Secretary to the Government of India, Ministry of Urban Development, on 16th March 1992, to Mr. C. Noronha, Vice Chairman, Delhi Development Authority regarding the order of the Urban Development Minister, Ms. Sheila Kaul, informing him that in the Delhi Master plan 1962, in Pinjrapole area (Andrews Gang), the land use of a plot of Nazul Land measuring about 35 acres was earmarked for housing, 18 acres zonal green and 17 acres for Community Center falling in Zone F-3 (Siri Fort Area). This question of land use of the pocket of land owned by Central Government Zone F-3 (Siri Area) described below was considered by the Government of India in 1989. The Central Government decided in 1989 that this pocket of land may be developed based on land use, as was existing in the Delhi Master Plan, 1962.

To meet the urgent need for accommodation for participants of the Afro-Asian Games, the work of land utilization as per the 1962 Master Plan was partially entrusted by the Government to the Central Public Works Department and partially to HUDCO. The Central Public Works Department was asked to construct type-IV quarters on 10 acres of land, and HUDCO was asked by the Government to develop and dispose of the Community Center on 17 acres of land, and out of the surplus proceeds, construct general pool quarters in 25 acres of land. The utilization of this land conforms with the provisions of the Delhi Master Plan, 1962.

When the layout plans for Community Center and a residential portion to be constructed by HUDCO were submitted to the Municipal Corporation of Delhi, the local body observed that in the revised Master Plan, the land use has been changed and is not in conformity with the land use assigned to the area in Master Plan for Delhi, 1962.

Land use of the pocket of land described above shall revert to the position which existed in the Delhi Master Plan, 1962, and the relevant zonal development plan: Residential and Zonal Green inadvertent - 53.60 acres and Community Center facing Khel Gaon Marg–17.60 acres.

The entire issue has been examined, and it is observed that when the Master Plan for Delhi 2001 was notified by the Government on 1st August 1990, there has been a bonafide error in omitting to specify the utilization of the above area in respect of Pinjrapole as per Delhi Master Plan, 1962, which resulted in an inadvertent change of land use of the area in question.

It has therefore been decided in the public interest to correct the bonafide mistake and restore the original land use, as was assigned to the plot in Pinjrapole (Andrews Ganj), to that as mentioned in Delhi Master Plan, 1962, i.e.,

35 acres for housing, 19 acres zonal green and 17 acres for Community Center.

Therefore, in the exercise of the powers conferred on the Central Government under Section 41 of the Delhi Development Act, 1957, the Central Government hereby directs the Delhi Development Authority to restore the land use of this area as existed for this land in the Master Plan for Delhi 1962 and process the change of land use by restoring to (i) Action u/s 11-A (2) for modification to the Master Plan for Delhi 2001, restoring with effect from 10th August 1990 the land use of the said area to that which existed in respect of this land in the Delhi Master Plan, 1962; (ii) Publish a Notice in such form and manner as prescribed by Delhi Development (Master Plan & Zonal Development Plan) Rules, 1959, inviting objections and suggestions from any person concerning proposed modification; and (iii) Follow such other procedures as is necessary to bring about the restoration of identified land use.

Accordingly, Mr. Pankaj Agrawala Dy. Secretary, Ministry of Urban Development through a letter dated 18th March 1992 addressed to Mr. G.R. Ambwani, Engineer of Chief,

Municipal Corporation of Delhi, referring to letter dated 19th February 1992 addressed to Mr. V. Suresh, Director Corporate Planning, HUDCO regarding the construction of HUDCO, Guesthouse cluster a & B at Andrews Gang– approval of layout plan and building plans:

In this regard, as you are aware, in the Delhi Master plan, 1962 in Pinjrapole area (Andrews Gang), in the land use of a plot of Nazul land measuring about 35 acres was earmarked for housing, 18 acres zonal green and 17 acres for Community Center. Out of this, an area measuring about 10 acres has been utilized by the Central Public Works Department for the construction of general pool residential accommodation. HUDCO has been asked by this ministry to develop and dispose of the Community Center, and out of the surplus proceeds, construct general pool quarters in 25 acres of land.

While notifying the Master Plan for Delhi, 2001, there has been a bonafide error of Pinjrapole, as per Delhi Master Plan, 1962. Necessary corrective action has been taken in this regard by issuing direction to Delhi Development Authority under Section 41 of the DD Act, 1957 for restoring the land use of the plot as it existed in the Delhi

Master Plan 1962 before 1st August 1990, when the Master Plan for Delhi 2001 was notified by the Central Government. Necessary action under Section 11A of the DD Act is being initiated by the Delhi Development Authority as per directions of the Central Government. In the meantime, you are requested to kindly formalize and approve the layout plan and building plans submitted by the HUDCO in respect of utilization in conformity with Delhi Master Plan 1962, subject to the provisions applicable to the plot as per the building bylaws and regulation on the subject, and forward the same to Delhi Urban Art Commission.

Another 695th meeting of Delhi Urban Art Commission was held on 20th March 1992, wherein the fresh plans submitted were otherwise considered satisfactory and approved conceptually. The architect was advised to route the proposal through a local body i.e., the Municipal Corporation of Delhi for the commission's formal consideration.

My observations as an author are that even though Delhi Urban Art Commission was aware of the land use under Master Plan, 1962, but they approved the concept of the layout containing the hotel part in the Community Center and the Guesthouses in the Community Center, as all the members were from the Ministry of Urban Development, and they had the pressure to do so. But to safeguard their approval, they sent to Municipal Corporation of Delhi to check that all is subject to the provisions applicable to the plot as per building bylaws and regulations on the subject and forward the same to Delhi Urban Art Commission.

Isn't it a scam that HUDCO proceeded to sell part of the land for the construction of the 5-Star Hotel despite the Municipal Corporation of Delhi and Delhi Development Authority objected to land use?

Chapter: Twenty-Four

First Allotment Letter Dated 27th March 1992 Issued by Land & Development Office to HUDCO for 32 Year Lease

It is on record as understood by me that the Land & Development Officer, despite the allotment letter by the Government to its office on 1st November 1990, had declined to issue the allotment letter to HUDCO as the land-use problem he was aware of. As the change of land use was sanctioned by the Minister of Congress Government, the Land & Development Office issued the allotment letter on 27th March 1992 to HUDCO for 32 years' lease at a premium of Re. 1/- per acre. The allotment letter was to be accepted by HUDCO, which was not accepted, nor were the lease fees paid. The Community Center was to be utilized for the development of Hostel and guesthouse facilities, conference hall, shopping & other Community Center facilities, as per the Urban Design for the complex approved by the Ministry of Urban Development.

Thus, the hotel use was not mentioned in the allotment letter which HUDCO as well as the Officers of the Ministry were aware of, as the hotel was considered a special use of the land. If no reply was received within 30 days from the date of receipt of the allotment letter, it was assumed HUDCO was not interested in the allotment, and the allotment was canceled at HUDCO's risk.

After it was decided and approved by the Minister of Urban Development for change of land use, the Land & Development Office at the Ministry of Urban Development issued a letter 27th March 1992 signed by Mr. Mahendra Sharma to Chairman-cum-Managing Director, HUDCO, allotting the land to the Housing & Urban Development Corporation Ltd. at Pinjrapole (Andrews Ganj, New Delhi).

I am directed to say that the President is pleased to sanction allotment of land measuring about 42.6 acres at Pinjrapole, Andrews, Ganj, New Delhi, as shown in Plan LDC No. 2403/2 in favor of HUDCO. The allotment is subject to the terms and conditions as given in the Memorandum of Agreement & Perpetual Lease, which shall also include:

i. The date of allotment of the site will be the date of this letter.
ii. HUDCO shall be required to construct the building in conformity with the architectural surroundings of the area within two years from handing over of the plot.
iii. 17.6 acres of land for the Community Center will be leased on payment of a token premium of Re. 1/-

and annual ground rent of Re. 1/- per acre for 32 years.

a. The land for the Community Center should be utilized for the development of Hostel and guesthouse facilities, conference hall, shopping & other Community Center facilities, as per the Urban Design for the complex approved by the Ministry of Urban Development. HUDCO will complete the construction of at least 100 houses/flats to be used temporarily by the Afro Asian Game Authorities before these Games are held in 1990-91. The construction plans shall be approved by the local body and Delhi Development Authority, Delhi Urban Art Commission, and the L&DO before undertaking any construction on the land.

iii. A review/monitoring Committee comprising Additional Secretary, Joint Secretary dealing with the Subject, and Joint Secretary (Finance) from the Ministry of Urban Development, and Chairman-cum-Managing Director, HUDCO will monitor/review the implementation of this project and will function as an Empowered Committee to take investment and disposal decisions as may be considered necessary for efficient completion of the project. Company Secretary, HUDCO will function as Secretary of this Committee.

iv. If the above terms and conditions are acceptable to the HUDCO, acceptance thereof in writing may please be communicated to the effect together with a check crossed 'Not Negotiable' for a sum of Rs. 75/- (Rs. Seventy-Five only) drawn in favor of the Land & Development Officer, New Delhi within 30 days from the date of receipt of this letter.

If no reply is received within 30 days from the date of receipt of this letter, it will be assumed you are not interested in the allotment, and the allotment will be canceled at your risk. Six copies of the present constitution of the HUDCO may also be furnished in this office.

Along with the letter dated 27th March 1992, a declaration under section 27 of the Urban Land Ceiling and Regulation

Act, 1976, was attached to be filled by HUDCO so that the permission under the Act could be applied for.

My observations are that HUDCO objected to the following terms of allotment dated 27th March 1992. The objections were submitted to the Land & Development Office on 5th May 1992, resulting in no allotment to HUDCO, unless HUDCO accepted an allotment letter for 32 years lease was recorded. HUDCO had no legal authority whatsoever. HUDCO did not even bother later or otherwise to fill the form under section 27 of the Urban Land Ceiling and Regulation Act, 1976, to obtain permission under the said Act.

Isn't it a Scam by non-acceptance by HUDCO of conditions of allotment letter to HUDCO by the Land & Development Office, despite the condition, the same was not canceled?

Chapter: Twenty-Five

Maneuvering Over the Terms of Allotment Letter Contrary to The Government Policies

It is observed by me as an author that HUDCO did not submit a layout plan for formal approval by the Delhi Urban Art Commission by sending it through the Municipal Corporation of Delhi, despite the reminders from the Delhi Urban Art Commission.

Delhi Urban Art Commission, Mr. M.B. Saxena, Secretary, through a letter dated 31st March 1992 reminded Mr. M.N. Joglakar, Executive Engineer HUDCO regarding at Pinjrapole (Conceptual Stage), that the plans were other rides considered satisfactory and approved conceptually. The architect was advised to route the proposal through the local body for the Commission's formal consideration. You are accordingly requested to route the scheme of the Pinjrapole, including the Transit Hostel, through the concerned local body for formal consideration of the Commission.

Mr. V Suresh HUDCO on 5th May 1992, in writing, placed the objections to Mr. Pankaj Aggarwal, Deputy Secretary (Lands) Ministry of Urban Development.

The Land & Development Office has issued a Letter No. L-II-1 (1974)/92/193 dated 27th March 1992, conveying the allotment of land at Andrews Ganj to HUDCO. This letter is in continuation of the Ministry's letter No. J-13014/6/90-LD, dated 1st November 1990 on the same subject, which is ongoing through this letter of L&DO, a certain point, as indicated in the statement, has been noticed. These points may please be looked into, and the allotment letter of L&DO suitably amended.

As you are aware, the Municipal Corporation of Delhi has raised a demand for Property Tax on HUDCO for this land. Any communication from the Ministry or L & DO gave rise to the presumption that the land in question has been allotted to HUDCO for its use may result in HUDCO's liability to pay the property tax, which may be about Rs. 2.00 crores to Rs.3.00 crores (US Dollar 11.57 million) per year. This may reduce the revenue available for the construction of General Pool Quarters. This point may be kept in view while issuing the revised allotment letter.

Various amendments sought by HUDCO in a letter dated 27th March 1992 were: Date of allotment - The date has been indicated as the date of issue of the letter, viz. 27th March 1992. HUDCO has already taken the site in question over, and the construction works are in progress. This condition will therefore have to be suitably modified, so that there may not be any objection that HUDCO have carried out the construction before the allotment. Period of Construction - It is indicated the construction shall be completed within two years after handing over the plot. Even the basic question, like a change of land use of this plot of land, is yet to be finalized. The period of construction should therefore be modified equitably. Payment of cost for Structure - there was no structure existing on this land, and HUDCO has already started construction in 1989-1990. This condition may therefore be removed.

The portions are shown for Community Center and Residential portions in the plan are not correct. In the Ministry's letter dated 1st November 1990, it was stated that separate communications will follow for leasing arrangements in the Community Center portion and a tenancy agreement between HUDCO and Government for the residential portion. These terms will have to be finalized quickly, and only after they are finalized, the allotment letter from L&DO may be issued incorporating these decisions. Also, with these decisions, it will not be possible to go ahead with the disposal of properties in the Community Center.

Regarding HUDCO's objections to certain terms in the allotment letter dated 27th March 1992 of Andrews Ganj land, Mr. G.V. Krishna Rau, Land & Development Officer dated 5th August 1992, considering the objections observed in his remarks in the noting putting before Higher Authorities proposing to agree to certain amendments sought by HUDCO in the allotment letter dated 27th March 1992. Date of allotment - the date of issue of the allotment letter was treated as the date of allotment as per practice. There is no harm in treating the date of taking possession by HUDCO as the date of allotment. However, the same is not available to us. If the HUDCO furnishes the date, we can suitably modify relevant clauses.

Period of Construction - As per the practice, two years are provided for completion of the construction, and the period is generally flexible depending on the requirements. Though HUDCO raised the change of the land use and accordingly requested for modifying the period, they are free to approach the Government for an extension of time if the present land use becomes a hindrance for the construction activity within the stipulated period. By their admission, the construction works are already, and the land used has not become a hindrance, and therefore, that cannot be the reason for modifying the time limit.

Though as usual, a clause indicating that the lease will be governed under the Government Grant Act was incorporated. Because of the special condition and relationship with HUDCO, we may agree with the contention of the HUDCO and delete this clause, since the allotment is not in reality for using HUDCO. It is in giving work to HUDCO to raise resources for general pool accommodation.

The terms & conditions for leasing arrangement need to be worked out separately by the Ministry with HUDCO. Since HUDCO specifically requested the revised allotment letter should be issued only after working out the terms and conditions of the leasing arrangement between the Government and HUDCO, perhaps these also may be finalized and communicated at the earliest to enable this office to issue the revised allotment letter.

Chapter: Twenty-Six

Steps Taken to Restore Land Use of Andrews Ganj Retrospectively to The Land Use as Per MPD 1962, Zone F-3, Allotment to HUDCO of Andrews Ganj Land Violated General Finance Rules 282 (3) Unless Approved by The Cabinet

All actions were taken to restore the land to Master Plan, 1962, to regularize the constructed buildings by HUDCO, so that the layout plans could be approved.

A public notice was issued in the Gazette of India Part-II Section-3, sub-section (ii) dated 23rd May 1992 referring to No. F-3 (33) 89-MP. Mr. Ranbir Singh issued this notice, Secretary, Delhi Development Authority: Public Notice:

The following modification which the Central Government proposes to assign to the Master Plan/Zonal Development Plan for Delhi is hereby published for public information. Any person having any objection or suggestion concerning the proposed modification may send the objection/suggestion in writing to the Secretary, Delhi Development Authority, Vikas Sadan within thirty days from the date of issue of this notice. The person making the objection or suggestion should also give his name and address.

Modification - The land use of an area measuring 28.75 hectares (71 acres) falling in zone F-3 (Pinjrapole), bounded by Government Pool Housing (Andrews Gang), Sadiq Nagar and Aryuvigyan Nagar, in the North and

South, Marshal J.B. Tittoo Marg 45 meters, wide (200 ft. r. w) in the East and Khelgaon road 30 meters, wise (100 r/w) in the west and earmarked in Master Plan for Delhi, 2001 for public and semi-public use (proposed convention center) is proposed to be restored to land uses earmarked in the composite zonal development plans of zones D-17, 18, 19, 20 and F-2 & 3, notified vide notification no. K-13012/7/71-UDI dt. 28.12.1973 i.e., for residential (housing)–14.17 hectare, commercial (Community Center)–6.88 hectare, and district parks/zonal green–7.70 hectare.

The plan indicating the proposed modification will be available for inspection at the office of the Deputy Director, Master Plan Section, Vikas Minar, 6th Floor, IP Estate, New Delhi on all working days within the period referred to above.

The Technical Committee meeting was held on 31st July 1992 by the Delhi Development Authority for change of land use, in which it was recorded:

The Secretary to the Government of India, Ministry of Urban Development, vide order no. K-20013/27/91-DDIB dated 16th March 1992 (Appendix-I) has conveyed the approval of the Central Government under section 11-A of the DD Act, 1957 to issue a public notice for inviting objection/suggestion from the public by exercising the powers conferred on the from the public by exercising the powers conferred on the Central Government under section 41 of the DD Act, 1957, and accordingly directed Delhi Development Authority to restore the land use of the proposed area as existed in 1962.

Accordingly, a public notice was issued on 23rd May 1992 for inviting public objections/suggestions. In response to that Public Notice, only one suggestion has been received. This is from the Joint Director (zonal planner), Delhi Development Authority. He has made the suggestions as under:

- The R.W. of Marshal Joship Broz Tittoo Marg is 60 m. (200 ft.)
- There is no such land use as 'zonal green' in the Master Plan for Delhi, 2001. (Appendix-II)'
- Observations–the R/W is 45 meters in the Master Plan for Delhi, 2001, and is mentioned the same.

The land use is shown as 'recreational' instead of the same.

- The proposal is placed before the Technical Committee for its consideration.

Decision–The technical Committee recommended to the Authority for approving the change of land use, and to refer to the Ministry of Urban Development to issue the notification under section 11 of the Delhi Development Act, 1957 for change of land use of an area measuring 28.75 hectares from public and semi-public facilities (Convention Center) to Community Center (Commercial use) 6.88-hectare Residential use 14.17 hectare and recreational use 7.70 hectares.

On 10th August 1992, change of land use of an area measuring 28.75 Ba. (71 acres) from 'Public and Semi-Public Facilities' (Convention Center) to Commercial, Residential, and Recreation use in the Pinjrapole area, New Delhi was discussed in the Delhi Development Authority Committee and item no. 81/92, file no. F.3 (33) 89-MP observed that in the Master Plan for Delhi, 2001, there is no land use as zonal green, therefore, Master Plan Land use needs to be indicated. Town Planner, Municipal

Corporation of Delhi, informed that there is no objection for the proposed modification from 'Public and Semi-Public Use' to part 'Residential. Part Commercial (Community Center) and Park District/Zonal Park.

The matter was placed before the Authority on 13th August 1992 for the consideration and approval of the Recommendations of the Technical Committee, and a resolution was passed by the Authority recommending to the Central Government the proposal for a change of land use of an area measuring 28.75 hact. (71 acres) from 'Public and Semi- Centre) 6.88 hact.; Residential use (Government Housing)-14.17 hact. and Recreational Use (7.7 hact).

In pursuance to the above, Mr. S.P. Jakhanwal from Delhi Development Authority informed on 10th August 1992 to Mr. R.K. Bhargava, Secretary to the Ministry of Urban Development, that in Pursuance of the Ministry of Urban Development reference No. K-20013/27/91-DDIB dated 16th March 1992 containing directions under SEC.41 of the Delhi Development Act, 1957, a Public Notice was issued inviting public objections/suggestions to change the land use of 28.75 Ha. Land in Pinjrapole/ Andrews Ganj. A copy of the resolution was sent with the letter to the Ministry for issuing the final Notification by the Government of India under Section 11 of the DD Act.

Mr. Anil Barai Deputy Director (Master Planning) also confirmed on 24th August 1992 to Mr. I.L. Bansal, Under Secretary Ministry of Urban Development, regarding change of land use, further stating that the Authority has approved/recommended the proposal vide its resolution number 109/92. It is therefore requested to issue a final notification for the proposed change of land use. Four copies of the location plan for authentication.
Isn't it a Scam if the land-use of Andrews Ganj 71 acres was restored retrospectively to Master Plan, 1962 land use in which hotel and Guesthouses were not allowed, could Community Center be used under Master Plan, 2001 as the Community Center as part of 71 acres?

In my view, the Government was aware of the violations of allotment to HUDCO, since the problems in the allotment letter to be issued to HUDCO were discussed for Andrews Ganj, as it required Cabinet approval and that the Public Sector Unit could not otherwise be given land for exploitation, and the arrangement with HUDCO needed to be approved by the Cabinet. But later, all these factors were ignored deliberately and intentionally, as the allotment of Andrews Ganj land to HUDCO was otherwise illegal unless regularized by the Cabinet.

A discussion was held on 5th August 1992 at 9.30 am of the high-level officers of the Ministry of Urban Development, in which the officers present were Mr. R. K Bhargava, Secretary, Mr. R. V Pillai, Additional Secretary, Mr. K. Dharmarajan, Joint Secretary (Urban Development), Dr. P.S. A Sundaram, Joint Secretary (HD), Mr. B. Bhattacharya, Joint Secretary (Finance), Mr. Pankaj Agrawala, Director (Land), Mr. B. R Dhiman, Desk Officer, Mr. K.K. Bhatnagar, Chairman-cum-Managing Director D, HUDCO, Mr. V. Suresh, Director (Corporate Planning), HUDCO in which the problems in the allotment of Andrews Ganj land were discussed, and a record note of discussion held on 5th August 1992 at 9.30 AM in the chamber of Secretary (Urban Development) regarding land as a resource for stepping up of investment in the construction of general pool accommodation were recorded on 12th August 1992:

Initiating the discussion, the secretary (Urban Development) mentioned that the main emphasis of the

Cabinet Note should be on the concept of the use of land as accommodation through public sector undertaking (PSU). A note must highlight the paucity of general pool accommodation (GPA) and the fact that despite the availability of suitable land, the accommodation cannot be constructed due to insufficient budgetary support. The secretary also highlighted the situation where there was a shortage of General Pool Accommodation on the one hand, and simultaneously the surplus land getting encroached on the other.

Any Public Sector Unit selected for the purpose would have to submit a plan of action on how it would exploit a given plot of land to generate surpluses. They would have to keep in mind the land use stipulated, its location, neighborhood, and environment, and based on this, they would be utilized for simultaneous construction of General Pool Accommodation. The Modalities of the plan would become a part of the memorandum of understanding between the PSU and the Government. The memorandum of understanding would contain inter alia financial arrangement, design specification of General Pool Accommodation and Construction, maintenance and transfer issues of General Pool Accommodation.

It was noted that the approval of the cabinet on the arrangement with HUDCO to the cabinet Note, as the allotment violated the General Finance Rules 282 (3).

Further, it was decided that instead of having a monitoring and review committee in respect of each project at the Government level, it is better if a memorandum of understanding is executed detailing all terms and conditions for execution of a particular project type of houses to be constructed, the time allowed for construction, handing over and maintenance, etc., and monitoring is done through the boards of the Public Sector Unit itself.

So far as maintenance of the General Pool Accommodation by Public Sector Unit is concerned, it was decided that in case the Central Public Works Department executes the construction as a deposit work, the Central Public Works Department will do the maintenance from the date of occupation of built-up accommodation. In case of a Public Sector Unit having done the construction, then it will maintain the building for 2 years from the date of occupation or up to the date of handing over to cover to the Central Public Works Department, whichever is earlier.

It was observed that the usual procedures followed by the Public Sector Unit for obtaining clearances for their projects through PIB would not be necessary, as the Public Sector Unit is acting as an agent of the Government and does not engage committee to examine the plan of the Public Sector Unit regarding optimal utilization of a given plot of land, could be constituted in which in addition to or their representatives not less than the rank of the joint secretary would-be members.

It was decided that after taking into consideration the views expressed above, a draft cabinet note will be prepared and finalized by the 10th instant.
Some issues relating to HUDCO were decided as per the following: -

The surplus generated should be simultaneously utilized for the construction of GPA. In case there is a gap when it is lying idle, it must be gainfully deposited in such accounts as would give the maximum returns.

HUDCO should take up the construction work of type IV, V quarters, and transit accommodation expeditiously. This could be done either by entrusting the work to the Central

Public Works Department on a deposit work basis or alternative arrangements through other PSUs involved, depending on the extent and capacity of the agencies to handle the work.

The designs for type IV. V and transit flats. Through cleared by the Ministry of Urban Development, monitoring and review committee should be put up for final approval, along with the internal furniture arrangement details, in participation of GD, the Central Public Works Department is also to be ensured considering a decision at 8 (A) Offer of Guesthouses to the central and state Government and PSU, etc., as per approved disposal policy, may be instituted forthwith. The meeting took note of the brochure brought out by HUDCO.

MUD should expedite notification of land use changes for the entire plot by taking it up with the Delhi Development Authority.

HUDCO should submit details of projected returns and cash flow, giving exact dates. They must also submit a detailed action plan.

HUDCO may also prepare a draft MOU, which should contain all the modalities of development, designing, financing, execution, transfer, and maintenance of the complete project. The meeting ended with a vote of thanks to the chair.

My dear readers, it must be decided whether the Ministry of Urban Development or HUDCO ever followed whether all the decisions made above, but such decisions were made as an eyewash in the files. The Officers of the Ministry continued to neglect such approval, as the same could not have been granted retrospectively, since HUDCO had already constructed the buildings illegally.

The Scams were high in 1992, and the other exposures of Scams shadowed the Scam of Andrew Ganj land since the Scam of Harshad Mehta & Ketan Parekh Stock Market Scam was highlighted in 1992 for Rs. 5000 Crore Combined, although not corruption scams, these had affected many people. There is no way that the investor community could forget the unfortunate Rs. 4000 crore Harshad Mehta scam and the over Rs. 1000 crore Ketan Parekh scam, which eroded the shareholders' wealth in an extensive market jolt.

Throughout financial history, investors have been defrauded from the Dutch Tulipmania to the South Sea bubble to the Mississippi Company scam. In recent history, stock scams have taken accounting fraud that cooks the books and hides losses to pyramid or Ponzi schemes for otherwise fictitious companies.

Harshad Mehta, the name that received its by-product as "the big bull", smashed to silicon after a mountainous property made entirely out of a scam considered the biggest and most magnificent stock market scam of all time. Who was Harshad Mehta? How did he become a name? How much mayhem did he cause in the stock market and trading? How skillfully did he dupe the entire system? How was he exposed?

The same is the story of Andrews Ganj land and HUDCO Scam, which has skillfully duped the private investor and is yet to be exposed. Isn't it a larger Scam than Harshad Mehta's scam?

Chapter: Twenty-Seven

Land Use of Andrews Ganj Notified Restoring to MPD 1962

The notification dated 8th September 1992 for change of land use of Andrews Ganj Land was sent to be issued by Mr. I.L. Bansal, Under Secretary (Deputy Director), Ministry of Urban Development, to the Manager, Government of India Press, Mayapuri, Ring Road, New Delhi.

NOTIFICATION

Whereas in the Delhi Master Plan, 1962, in Pinjrapole (Andrews Ganj) area, the land use of a Nazul land measuring about 35 crores was earmarked for housing, 1-acre zonal green, and 17 acres for Community Center.

Whereas to meet the urgent need for accommodation for participants of the Afro-Asian Games, as per the land use in Master Plan for Delhi-62, a portion of land measuring about 10 acres had been entrusted by the Government to the Central Public Works Department for the construction of Type-IV quarters, and another portion had been entrusted to HUDCO for construction of Community Center on 17 acres and General Pool Quarters on 25 acres.

A bonafide error had occurred while notifying the Master Plan for Delhi, 2001 by the Government on 1/8/90 in as much as the land use of the aforesaid area, which was to continue to conform with the Master Plan for Delhi, 1962, was omitted to be mentioned as such, resulting in an inadvertent change of land use of the aforesaid area.

The Central Government directed Delhi Development Authority in the public interest to restore the land use of the aforesaid, as mentioned in the Delhi Master Plan, 1962.

The proposed modification was published with Notice N. F.3 (33) 89-MP dated 23/5/92 following the provisions of section 44 of the Delhi Development Act (61 of 1957), inviting objections/suggestions as required by sub-section (3) of Section 11-A of the said Act, within thirty days from the date of the said notice.
AND WHEREAS no objection/suggestions have been received concerning the proposed modification.

NOW, therefore, in the exercise of the powers conferred by sub-section (2) of section 11-A of the said Act, the Central Government hereby makes the following modification in the said Master Plan for Delhi with retrospective effect.

Modification - The land use of an area measuring 28.75 ha. (71 acres) falling in Zone F-3 (Pinjrapole Area) bounded by Government Pool Housing (Andrews Ganj), Sadiq Nagar and Ayurvigyan Nagar, in the North and South, Marshal J.B. Tito Marg 45 meters wide R/W in the East and Khel Gaon Road 30 meters. Wide in the West and earmarked in Master Plan for Delhi, 2001 for public and semi-public use' (proposed-convention center)' is restored to land uses earmarked in the composite zonal development plans of Zones D-17, 18,19 20 and F-2&3, notified vide Notification No. K-13012/7/71-UDI dated 28/12/73, i.e., for "residential" (housing)–14.17 ha. "Commercial (Community Center)–6.88 ha. and "district parks/zonal green–7.70 ha."

Table 3: Shopping and other facilities, and the various Tiers of Planning Areas for Zone F-3

Pop. 1,50,000 - 2,500,000	Pop. 40,000-50,000	Pop. 12,000–15,000	Pop. 3,500–5,000	Pop. 20–1,000
DISTRICT CENTRES	COMMUNITY CENTER	RESIDENTIAL PLANNING AREA	RESIDENTIAL UNIT	HOUSING CLUST
Shopping 200 to 350 shops, facilities, and service industries and Government officers	No. of shops 80 to 100, library, religious buildings. Cinemas Petrol Pump (Service Garage) Shopping and Service Industries: professional officers, health center, post	Local Shopping: 15 to 20 retails shops plus service shops, professional officers Community Hall, High School, Parks	Convenience shopping No. of shops 4 to 6 Primary School Playground	Toilets Nursery School

	office and Telegraph Office, Telephone Exchange, Police Station, Fire Station and Electric Sub-Station			

Table 4: Distribution of retail shopping areas in Zonal Development Plans

Site Residential deputy	Community Center (Including shopping, services industries and garages, community facilities	Residential Planning area center of local shopping (including community hall)	Convenience shopping in residential units (only shopping)			

p.p. a	Acres	No. of Shops	Acres	No. of Shops	Acres	No. of Shops
21	15.00	50 to 100	1.75	15 to 20	0.50	4 to 6
50	13.0	Do	1.50	Do	0.50	Do
60	12.0	Do	1.30	Do	0.50	Do
75	10.0	Do	1.20	Do	0.40	Do
100	8.0	Do	1.10	Do	0.30	Do
125	7.0	Do	0.90	Do	0.30	Do
150	7.0	Do	0.90	Do	0.30	Do
200	6.0	Do	0.80	Do	0.20	Do

Mrs. Manju Safaya, Senior Design Officer, HUDCO circulated the minutes on 23rd September 1992 of the meeting with all the consultants of Andrews Ganj Housing Project held on 16th September 1992 at 4 pm in which the officers present were Mr. K.K. Bhatnagar–Chairman-cum-Managing Director, HUDCO, Mr. V. Suresh–Director Corporate Planning HUDCO, Mr. MN Joglekar–Executive Director, HUDCO, Mr. K.C. Batra–PCA HUDCO, Mr. N. Rajagopalan–Consultant, HUDCO, Mrs. Manju Safaya–Senior Design Officer (A), HUDCO, Mr. Ravindra Bhan–Consultant, Architect, Mr. Vasant Kamanth–Architect, Mr. Navin Gupta & Mr. V.S. Rawat–Representatives of Architect Mr. Gauram Bhatia, Mr. Kailash Aggarwal & Mr. Sanjay Kumar–Representatives of consultant Architects Mr. S.K. Das, it was discussed:

Obtaining approval–At the outset, Chairman-cum-Managing Director, HUDCO thanked all the consultant Architect for attending the meeting and requested Mr. Jasbir Sawhney, Prime Consultant, to appraise the meeting regarding the latest status for approval of the layout plan from Delhi Urban Art Commission/local bodies. Mr. Sawhney explained since the clearance for retaining the land use as per MP-1962 is awaited from Delhi

Development Authority, and the issue relating to the location of the substation is yet to be sorted out with Delhi Electricity Supply Undertaking, the formal approval from the Municipal Corporation of Delhi is pending Director Corporate Planning.

HUDCO informed the Ministry of Urban Development already issued a notification, and the location of the substation is being sorted out. Therefore, it was decided the consultant can obtain approval from the Delhi Urban Art Commission on the layout by 30th September 1992.

After discussion, it was decided that approval be obtained on the layout plan already submitted to the Municipal Corporation of Delhi & forwarded by them to Delhi Urban Art Commission. It was decided as soon as Delhi Urban Art Commission forwards the plan to the Municipal Corporation of Delhi for formal approval, the revised layout along with all the housing designs can be submitted for conceptual approval from Delhi Urban Art Commission.

All the housing consultants welcomed the decision and agreed for submitting the building plans for approval from the Delhi Urban Art Commission. However, it was requested HUDCO/Mindor of Urban Development give the final approval on their designs. Director Corporate Planning, HUDCO informed that a presentation of all the design reflecting furniture layout to the Secretary, Ministry of Urban Development, is being fixed up, whereby the design will be frozen.

Action required by Joint Secretary	Action required by all the Consultant		
Stage	Time Schedule	Stage	Time Schedule
Approval of layout plan from Delhi Urban Art Commission	30th September 1992	Informal clearance from Municipal Corporation of Delhi-Building section for individual housing designs	30th September 1992
Submission of revised layout plan to Delhi Urban Art Commission	1st October 1992	Submission of the building design for conceptual approval from Delhi Urban Art Commission	1st October 1992

Formal approval of layout from Municipal Corporation of Delhi-Town Planning Department, CFO, Civil Aviation, etc.	One month	Start preparation of working drawings/estimates	15th October 1992
		Submission of building design to Municipal Corporation of Delhi-Building Section	31st October 1992
		Final preparation of detailed working drags/estimates for floating tenders	15th December 1992
		Tender inviting	15th January 1993
		Work awarded commencement of work	31st January 1993

Mr. Anil Barai, Deputy Director (Master Planning), informed HUDCO on 9th October 1992 regarding changed the land use of an area measuring 28.75 ha. (71 ACRES) from Public and Semi-Public Facilities (Convention Center) to residential'-14.17 ha. Commercial' (Community Center)- 6.88ha and district parks and zonal green'-7.70 ha. At Pinjrapole Scheme, New Delhi forwarding a copy of Notification no. K-20013/27 1–DDIB dated 8th September 1992 on the subject noted above, issued by the Under Secretary to the Government of India, Ministry of Urban Development, for information. Further, requested HUDCO to send a copy of the layout plan duly indicating proposed sites.

In my view, the Government was forced to notify the land-use change on 8th September 1992 retrospectively, as per the Master Plan, 1962. This led to another disaster, as the residential complex could be regularized, but the land use of the Community Center as per Master Plan, 1962 did not permit the construction of the Guesthouses or the use of land for the hotel. Since HUDCO had already made heavy investments in the construction of guesthouse blocks, the Government and HUDCO were constrained to propose to sell the properties without any approval of the building plans. Thus, HUDCO and Government Officers jointly brought the concept of selling the properties without disclosing the fact that the buildings were constructed unauthorized and without the approval of building plans. HUDCO and the Government represented by its Minister and the Officers of the Ministry of Urban Development were hands in glove, and they proposed to bring a new concept in disclosing in the brochure "the Government approves the Urban Design. This concept was proposed to be published to make fools of the investors and to allure them to buy the properties by keeping the reserve price at higher values.

No investor in the properties could ever believe the properties constructed by HUDCO on the directions of the Ministry of Urban Development could be illegal, and even the layout plan had not been approved when the properties at Andrews Ganj were being sold by HUDCO from 1992 onward.

HUDCO created an aura by taking the name of the Government to market the illegal properties. HUDCO also brought a new concept with the Ministry of Urban Development that the land for the hotel is "Earmarked for Hotel in the Envelope Area", knowing that the Community

Center, as notified under Zone F-3 under Master Plan, 1962, could not be used for the hotel.

My dear readers, wasn't it a deceptive scheme leading to a scam by HUDCO and the then Government?

Chapter: Twenty-Eight

HUDCO Concealed Several Facts About the Illegal Constructions and Called for Bids for Guest House Blocks in October 1992

In my view, and as per records, HUDCO and Ministry of Urban Development, officers at the end of 1992 and beginning of 1993 were aware that the entire buildings constructed at Andrews Ganj were illegal, as even the layout plan had not been submitted due to a change of land use done on 8th September 1992. They were also aware that in the Community Center, land use of the hotel was not permitted, but they continued to plan the part of the sale of Andrews Ganj land for the hotel. This was resulting in a further scam by the Ministry and the HUDCO knowingly that the land use for the hotel is not permitted as per Master Plan, 1962, to which the land was restored, and nothing could be utilized in the 71 acres land at Andrews Ganj as per Master Plan, 2001.

Municipal Corporation of Delhi sent the reminder on 13th October 1992 to Mr. Jasbir Sawhney to comply with the notice sent regarding Andrews Ganj project for considering layout plan with revised layout plan as per Master Plan, 1962, and the Community Center uses should also be as per Zone F-3 under Master Plan, 1962.

HUDCO construction wing on 14th October 1992, placed its concerns regarding Issue relating to the HUDCO Place integrated Project at Andrews Ganj, requiring urgent attention as the constructions were already completed of all the buildings:

The Urban design for the remaining portion of the Community Center is to be finalized by Mr. Jasbir Sawhney to enable him to take up the Community Center planning/design work. The presentation of the layout plan for Zonal Green, as finalized by Mr. Sahir for Landscape Consultant, is required to be delivered to the Government Monitoring and Review Committee, and Secretary, Ministry of Urban Development, for approval.

The plans for various pockets of General Pool Quarters with furniture layout duly incorporated are to be presented to the Government Monitoring and Review Committee and Secretary Urban Development for approval. DG, Central Public Works Department, also is to participate in this presentation, as desired by Secretary Urban Development in the meeting.

Follow-up action of the Minutes of the meeting held by Chairman-cum-Managing Director with all Consulting Architects of Andrews Ganj Project on 16th September

1992, especially concerning the approval of layout plan and other statutory approvals to be obtained by Mr. Jasbir Sawhney, the Consulting Architect from, Delhi Urban Art Commission, Municipal Corporation of Delhi, Delhi Electricity Supply Undertaking, Delhi Water Supply Undertaking, Fire Authorities, Civil Aviation, etc.

Director Corporate Planning may kindly see and indicate the present position of the above issues.

In pursuance, HUDCO's Director Corporate Planning directed Mrs. Manju Safaya, Senior Design Officer, to get the status who inquired on 14th October 1992 the present position of Mr. Jasbir Sawhney, Architect telephonically on the points made by the Construction Wing, and submitted on 15th October 1992 that as desired, the present position as on today:

The Joint Secretary will be making a brief present action in the meeting to be held on 19th October 1992 at 2.30 pm in Chairman-cum-Managing Director's chamber. Mr. Sahir, Landscape Consultant, is long back ready with designs for a presentation in the Ministry of Urban Development. All the consultants are ready with the furniture layout for a housing project. By 20th October, they will submit the drawings to HUDCO.

As per discussion with Mr. Jasbir Sawhney Architect, all or any approval is impossible until No Objection Certificate from Delhi Electricity Supply Undertaking is obtained. Only after the site for sub-station is marked on the layout as per the Delhi Electricity Supply Undertaking requirement, the formal approval for the Delhi Urban Art Commission will be given and drawings sent back to the Municipal Corporation of Delhi for its approval.

The various stages for approval of layout building plans now are indicated below:

Delhi Electricity Supply Undertaking Sub-Station>>Delhi Urban Art Commission Layout Approval>> Municipal Corporation of Delhi Layout Approval >> Municipal Corporation of Delhi Building Plan submission>> Municipal Corporation of Delhi Building Plan Approval>> Firefight Approval >>Delhi Water Supply and Sewerage Board

Therefore, a meeting of Director Corporate with Delhi Electricity Supply Undertaking or any other high-level official from Delhi Electricity Supply Undertaking with Chairman-cum-Managing Director HUDCO may be fixed up at the earliest to avoid further delay, please.

HUDCO floated a brochure in September 1992 calling for the bids on 15th October 1992 for Guesthouses by creating an attractive brochure without disclosing that the guesthouses had no sanctions of building plans and that the layout plan of Andrews Ganj was still not approved. HUDCO in the brochure:

HUDCO PLACE

- Guesthouses
- A Unique Urban Experience
- Khel Gaon Marg, Andrews Ganj, New Delhi
- HUDCO Place
- A Unique Urban Experience

INTEGRATED URBAN DESIGN

Housing and Urban Development Corporation Ltd. under the direction of the Government of India. The Ministry of Urban Development is developing HUDCO Place, designed and developed as an integral Urban Design complex with design controls, graphic signage, landscape, parking, and other common services. It is a perfect blend of traditional ambiance and up-to-date modern facilities. A spacious Central Plaza has been designed to create an environment of social interaction. A Five-Star Hotel, a low-budget hotel, an air-conditioned and Shopping Arcade, and a Cultural Centre and the highlights of this integrated urban complex. The street and codes will be interspersed with restaurants, shops, and art galleries. The two Guesthouse clusters on either side of the Central Plaza are designed as self-contained units with facilities comparable to Star Hotel.

LOCATION

Located in the heart of South Delhi, within a stone's throw of Siri Fort, HUDCO Place is spread over 17.5 acres of land in the Andrews Ganj area. Flanked by Khelgaon Marg and Josip Broz Tito Marg. HUDCO Place lies midway between Ring Road and Outer Ring Road, making it eminently accessible for the location of Guesthouses.

LANDSCAPE

An 18-acre stretch of land demarcated as a Green Zone with parks, fountains, and water bodies lies in the vicinity of HUDCO PLACE, offering an added attraction.

PROPOSED BUILD-UP AREA

The total built-up area, according to the urban design, will be about 71,700 sq. of which 27,500 Sq. have been earmarked for the Guesthouse blocks. The Guesthouses have been designed in two clusters of six blocks, each with pedestrian landscaped spaces within and a road on the periphery, the blocks being four-storied.

Each four-storied block consists of an average of 40 rooms on three floors, with a ground floor comprising an entrance lobby, restaurant, shops, and service areas.

The cluster approach to urban design has been a deliberate choice, following the dictates of urban form and the need to achieve a high density notwithstanding the low-rise structures. The guesthouse rooms are placed around an internal courtyard.

CONSTRUCTION

The first phase of the construction will focus on the Guesthouse clusters. The structural works have already been completed, and this part of the complex is expected to be completed by December 1992. The buildings will conform to all statutory requirements and will maintain high environmental standards.

SPECIFICATIONS

The Guesthouses are finished in permanent material using machine-made bricks, with blue glass mosaic and tiles on the rooftop. The glazed doors and windows are in anodized aluminum. The internal doors have teakwood frames with block board shutters. The rooms are finished in ceramic tiles on the floor and wall, while the flooring of the lobby and other areas is in marble, etc., depending on interior designs.

FACILITIES

With due regard for the economy in capital expenditure, energy, and maintenance costs, the services provided at the complex will be centralized, thereby ensuring greater efficiency in the systems. These services include:

- Air conditioning plant
- Boilers
- Electric substation
- Standby diesel generator sets.
- Water Storage and pumping
- Telephone Exchange

FACILITIES AT GUESTHOUSES

All the rooms at the Guesthouses are centrally air-conditioned, with attached bathrooms running hot and cold water, and are equipped with telephone connections. Adequate provisions have been made in the Community Center complex for Shopping Arcades, shopping malls, Cultural centers, Restaurants, Coffee shops, Swimming pools, and Beauty Parlor. Parks. Gardens and facilities for art display are a part of the general scene.

Conveniently placed underground parking is being provided in a Central Plaza accessible from all parts of the urban design complex.

INTERIORS

Each guesthouse block interior has been designed with a distinct and individual finish. Care has been taken to maintain a high aesthetic quality in the design reflecting a sense of creativity and artistic conception.

Standard guest room of one bay: This room is based on about 15 Sq. room area, with an additional area for the bathroom and vestibule area for the cupboard.

One and a half bay suite: This is a larger room, providing a separate space for a bed and sitting area, and equivalent to about 1.5 times the room area of the standard guest room. The bathroom and vestibule are in general like the standard room.

Two bay Suite: These are suites having a regular standard guesthouse, a bathroom and vestibule area, and an additional sitting room.

Installments: (i) At the time of allotment 15% (ii) Within 3 months of allotment 50% (iii) On completion of finishes 25% (iv) At the time of possession 10%.

DISPOSAL TERMS

The rooms will be given on long terms first for 30 years, with two renewable leases also of 30 years each.

Apart from the price, the lessees shall pay 2.5% of the premium as Annual Ground Rent.

The Registration of the Lease/Sale Deed shall be as per the laws applicable in the Union Territory of Delhi. The Stamp Duty cost and other charges in this respect will be borne by the lessees.

Transfer of leasehold interest and/or property will require prior permission of the lessor.

The other terms of the lease shall be as decided by the lessor, and generally on such lines as the leases entered by L & DO/ Delhi Development Authority.

Application with bank drafts must reach on or before 15th October 1992.

There was not much response, although HUDCO concealed several facts about the illegal constructions and claimed the buildings will be complete by December 1992, thinking that they will have the plans approved by then, although the constructions were already completed, they placed a picture in the brochure as if the constructions were at the final stage. In the brochure, they had also stated the 32 years lease will be renewed two times, i.e., for 30 years before the expiry of the lease. These were not the terms of allotment by the Land & Development officer to HUDCO. But HUDCO along with the Ministry were involved in alluring the buyers to sell the properties somehow.

Wasn't it a fraudulent scheme to sell Guesthouse Blocks in 1992, which had no sanction of building plans when the Architect had given the various stages for approval of layout building plans: Delhi Electricity Supply Undertaking Sub- Station>>Delhi Urban Art Commission Layout Approval>> Municipal Corporation of Delhi Layout Approval >> Municipal Corporation of Delhi Building Plan submission>> Municipal Corporation of Delhi Building Plan Approval>> Firefight Approval >>Delhi Water Supply and Sewerage Board?

Isn't it a Scam the brochure was floated without disclosure of the illegal buildings and seeking 65% of the money towards the property within three months?

The illegal constructions at Andrews Ganj were carried out between 1989 and 1992 without any building plan approvals, without Fire Safety approvals, without electric connection, without the water supply, sewerage, and drainage plan approvals, etc. The Government through the Ministry of Urban Development was in a much more controlled situation of HUDCO, who owned the company. Both of them agreed to conceal the real and the facts of Andrews Ganj's project to collect monies illegally by concealing various facts, resulting in fraud and cheating the investor who would ever come in to purchase these properties.

HUDCO and the Government of India needed to disclose all the facts, but they were desperate to realize the monies invested by HUDCO in the construction of Guesthouse Blocks at the Community Center and the car park basement constructed in the Community Center all illegally without any approvals. The Government officials of the Ministry of Urban Development could have not approved the building plans or the Fire safety measurements required to be followed in constructing these properties, which was the job of the Municipal Corporation of Delhi and Fire Department.

HUDCO worked as a mediator for the Government to get the monies by essential non-disclosures and both worked together hand in hand to cheat the investor to buy these properties. Meanwhile, three parties had already developed a keen interest in buying or investing in the properties at Andrews Ganj, and three interested parties were Phoenix, MS Shoes[4], and Asian Hotels, who were ready to jump into investing in these properties.

---

[4] (Ms. Shoes East Ltd vs Housing & Urban Development ... on 3 July, 2010, 2010)

Chapter: Twenty-Nine

Empowered Committee of Government Abolished Giving All Powers to HUDCO

The response received against the brochure for Guesthouses was from some public sector companies and state-owned companies. HUDCO issued the allotment letters in January 1993 to the Government of Karnataka. HUDCO had represented on 3rd November 1992 to the Ministry of Urban Development to its Joint Secretary Mr. K. Dharmarajan regarding the viability of the hotel project and the reserve price fixed by HUDCO, who in return on 25th November 1992 confirmed to Mr. K.K. Bhatnagar, Chairman-cum-Managing Director of HUDCO:

In the light of the explanation thereon, the Ministry has no objection to the reserve price fixed by HUDCO. As regards the pre-qualification category and recovery of part of the payment in foreign exchange, your attention is drawn to the minutes of the meeting held on 8th October 1992 and subsequent clarification issued in this. You may act accordingly. As regards the percentage of built-up space that could be allowed for commercial use, we may go by the stipulation of the Master Plan for Delhi, 2001.

You are requested to expedite the disposal of various commercial sites in the 17.5 acres of land earmarked for the Community Center to generate sufficient resources to construct general pool residential accommodation in the remaining 25 acres of the project area. I shall be grateful if you could indicate the total surplus that is likely to be generated in this venture, and the number of residential accommodation type-wise that would be constructed from utilizing the surplus, and the time frame for the construction. This would enable the Ministry of Urban Development to enter into a suitable MOU with HUDCO for this project.

A meeting was held on 15th December 1992 at 10.00 A.M. in the conference room under the Chairmanship of the Secretary (Urban Development) to consider the role of the Review & Monitoring Committee constituted concerning Pinjrapole, Andrews Ganj Project. The members present were Mr. R.K. Bhargava, Secretary (Urban Development)- In Chair, Mr. C.D. Tripathi -Additional Secretary, K. Dharmarajan, Joint Secretary (Urban Development), Dr. P.S.A. Sundaram, Joint Secretary (HD), Mrs. A. Ahluwalia, Financial Advisor (Urban Development) Pankaj Agrawala, Director (Land) and B.R. Dhiman, Under Secretary (Land) Mr. K.K. Bhatnagar, Chairman-cum-Managing Director, Mr. V. Suresh, Director (Corporate Planning) in which it was decided:

In the light of the notice giving a brief of the subject matter and related provisions in the proposal being submitted for consideration of the Cabinet regarding land as a resource for stepping up investment in the construction of the General Pool Accommodation, after detailed deliberations on the subject matter, it was believed:

Since working of the HUDCO is controlled through the Board of Directors, in which Joint Secretary (HD) & Joint Secretary (Finance) are members, the need for having a review & monitoring committee for the Pinjrapole project was reviewed, and it was believed once a memorandum of understanding detailing terms & conditions for execution of the project, its disposal policy, and the surplus generated and type of houses to be constructed, a time allowed for construction/handing over and arrangements for maintenance, etc. The executing agency should have the freedom to take investment & policy decisions through or under the authority of its Board of Directors.

In the light of (1) above, it was decided that keeping in view the terms & conditions of allotment, the memorandum prepared by the HUDCO, draft Memorandum of Understanding should be finalized detailing the background as well as the areas covered so far and the items yet to be accomplished.

After the execution of the Memorandum of Understanding, the HUDCO will be required to furnish a monthly progress report to enable the Government to watch the progress of the conditions spelled out in the MOU.

Accordingly, Chairman-cum-Managing Director, HUDCO was requested to urgently prepare a Memorandum of Understanding for execution between the Government and the HUDCO. After execution of the MOU, the review & monitoring committee will cease to function, and the HUDCO will take investment & disposal decisions. The meeting ended with a vote of thanks to the Chair.
In pursuance of the decision of the Ministry of Urban Development to wind up the Government Monitoring & Review Committee on Andrews Ganj Project and enter into a Memorandum of Understanding between Government & HUDCO was placed before the board of HUDCO, it was decided that on receipt of these Minutes a reply has been sent to the Ministry indicating that since the execution of the MOU identifying the various issues stated in the Minutes would take some more time; it is hoped the

Government Monitoring & Review Committee would continue to function since important policy issues relating to disposal of properties have to be resolved, the Ministry has been informed we shall be shortly sending the Agenda Items and notes or the meeting of the Committee.

HUDCO succeeded to abolish the Empowered Monitoring Committee for Andrews Ganj project, based on the directions of the Minister of Congress Government through the Secretary of the Ministry of Urban Development, to get the power on the entire Andrews Ganj land. From here, further scams by HUDCO started as independently as a corporation could be, especially under the director corporate who was handling this project. But to act smoothly, I still wrote to the Ministry to continue the Committee until the MOU is decided.

Given the fact, it was a final decision of the ministry that working of the HUDCO is controlled through the Board of Directors, in which joint Secretary of the ministry and Joint Secretary finance from the ministry of finance is the member's disposal policy, and the surplus generated and type of houses to be constructed, the time allowed for construction/handing over, and arrangements for maintenance, etc. have been finalized. The executing agency HUDCO was given the freedom to take investment & policy decisions through or under the authority of its Board of Directors.

It is important to note that the HUDCO board was given all the powers, but at times whenever it suited to ministry, HUDCO's board had no power to decide, and on the other side, after HUDCO's board would decide, then if suited to HUDCO, it was said they needed the approval of the ministry. All were played in as per their conveniences as well as their whims.

Wasn't it a Scam abolishing the Empowered Committee of the Government, which was a precondition of the allotment and all the powers given to HUDCO in respect of Andrews Ganj land?

The Government was worried the investments made by HUDCO in constructing these buildings are being charged @ 17% interest, as agreed by them. Both were worried about the disposal of these properties from 1992 onward itself when various efforts to sell failed. The government had validated the fact of unauthorized constructions, since in between on 1st August 1990, the land use of Andrews Ganj was notified as Convention Center, and the land was to be used for institution purposes. But HUDCO had carried out constructions as per Master Plan, 1962 of the residential buildings constructed on 25-acre land part of the Andrews Ganj land, and the Community Center was being used as per Master Plan, 2001, which was wrong and illegal.

Chapter: Thirty

All Powers for Disposal Decision of Andrews Ganj Land Given to CMD, HUDCO

In my view, HUDCO succeeded to get various conditions amended of allotment letter dated 27th March 1992 issued by the Land & Development Officer to HUDCO, which were contrary to the Government Policies to give land to public sectors.

Under Secretary, Mr. B.R. Dhiman, to the Ministry of Urban Development in writing on 28th December 1992 to Land and Development Officer with a copy to Chairman-cum-Managing Director, HUDCO regarding the allotment of land to Housing and Urban Development Corporation Ltd., at Pinjrapole (Andrews Ganj) New Delhi:

I am directed to refer to the correspondence resting with this Ministry's letter of even number dated the 1st November 1990, and to say that the matter has been examined in the light of the points raised by HUDCO vide their letters No. HUDCO/EM/Andrews/91 dated 5th May 1992 and D. O. letter No. HUDCO/DEP/M & RG/92 dated 3rd July 1992 & L&DO's U.O. No. L. II-1 (974)/90 dated 11th August 1992. Accordingly, the relevant paragraphs of the allotment letter were replaced:

Para 4: A Memorandum of the undertaking will be executed between the Government of India & HUDCO, detailing the terms and conditions for execution of the project, type of houses to be constructed, the time allowed for construction, handing over, arrangements for maintenance, etc. The monitoring of day activities related to the project would be done by or under the authority of the board of directors of the HUDCO. After execution of the MOU, the HUDCO would be required to submit a monthly progress report relating to the project, to enable the Government to watch the progress of the project to ensure fulfillment of the targets, terms, and conditions spelled out in the MOU.

The points raised by the HUDCO concerning the allotment letter issued by the L&DO on 27th March 1992 are clarified as under:

i. Date of allotment

The date of allotment should be the date of issue of the letter by the Ministry, i.e., 1-11-1990

ii. Period of construction.

The construction should be completed within two years from the date of handing over of the plot, or within such an extended period as decided by the Government.

THE DIRECTOR MINISTRY

The area allocated for construction of General Pool accommodation, as well as the development of the Community Center, should be correctly indicated in the plan after ascertaining the utilization proposed by HUDCO.

HUDCO's director, Mr. V. Suresh, through a letter dated 4th January 1993 to the Director Ministry of Urban Development referring to communication No. J-13014/6/90-LD dated 28th December 1992 conveying the record note of discussion held on 15th December 1992 on the subject of review & monitoring on the Andrews Ganj Project.

Since the execution of the MOU identifying the various issues as of the Record Notes, it would take some more time. It is hoped the review & monitoring committee of the Ministry of Urban Development would continue to dispose of properties that have to be resolved. We shall be shortly sending agenda items and notes for a meeting of the committee. However, no agenda was sent nor the meeting of the Monitoring was held.

HUDCO in their 159th board meeting, Item 159.2.12, decided that the Committee of Directors may be authorized to take all decisions relating to the management of the project, including the approval of tenders. The definition of the scope of functions and powers of the Committee of Directors does not include taking decisions relating to the disposal of properties. It is therefore considered necessary that a specific delegation of powers to the Committee of Directors is required from the Board of Directors to take decisions regarding disposal and regularize other aspects of disposal.

It may also be indicated here that a decision has been taken by the Ministry of Urban Development to discontinue the Government Monitoring and Review Committee and enter into a Memorandum of Understanding between Government and HUDCO. After the signing of the Memorandum, the Government Monitoring and Review Committee ceases to exist, and the investment and disposal decision will be taken by the Directors of HUDCO. A copy of the Minutes containing the decision is placed before the board. It is, therefore, necessary that the level at which such decisions are to be taken is clearly defined.

The board decided to authorize the Committee of Directors on Project Management to take disposal decisions, including fixation of the prices, and regularize other aspects of disposal based on the recommendations of the Government Monitoring and Review Committee until it existed, and thereafter, based on the contents of the MOU signed between Government and HUDCO. Ratify the action taken so far for disposal of guesthouse space and hotel site at HUDCO Place, Andrews Ganj. Authorize Chairman-cum-Managing Director to take all necessary action in pursuance of the disposal decisions taken by the Committee of Directors.

It was decided that well-established companies have collaboration agreements with well-known companies of hotels in India and/or abroad, including foreign companies and non-resident Indians. The offer shall be divided into two parts, i.e., technical & financial, along with an earnest money deposit of Rs. One lakh financial bid shall be opened only in those cases where the offer is found to be technically competent. The last date of submission of the offer would be 28th February 1993.

HUDCO further decided while disposing of the Hotel Site at HUDCO Place, Andrews Ganj, to set up the Scrutiny Committee to scrutinize the bids and take decisions, etc.

Isn't it a scam that without any land use of the hotel and approval of the layout plans of Andrews Ganj, HUDCO decided to dispose of the 5-Star Hotel site at HUDCO Place Andrews Ganj, New Delhi?

Chapter: Thirty-One

HUDCO's Representation to Change Lease Period from 32 Years to 99 Years to Realize More Money

In my view, as an author, since HUDCO attempted various times to dispose of the properties at Andrews Ganj, Community Center constructed illegally Guesthouses, as well as the proposed hotel on 3 acres, shopping arcade on the illegal basement constructed by HUDCO, and 2500 sq. meters. Cultural Centre. HUDCO had attempted in 1992 to sell the hotel land at the first instance by writing to various hotels & business houses. The offer was received in 1992 from Asian Consolidated Industries Limited, the terms of which were vague and doubtful.

HUDCO represented to the Government, Ministry of Urban Development, that the realization of the properties for 32 years lease would be much less when Delhi Development Authority is issuing allotment for 99 years. It may be considered changing the lease period from 32 years to 99 years to exploit the receipt of maximum amounts from the Community Center. The proposal was under active consideration by the Ministry of Urban Development, as the Government, as well as HUDCO, were greedy to receive maximum amounts even if non-disclosures in the brochure are created.

HUDCO held a 177th board meeting on 2nd February 1993, in which in item 2.6 the disposal of the properties at Community Center, Andrews Ganj was discussed and decided based on the decision of the Ministry of Urban Development to wind up the Government Monitoring & Review Committee on Andrews Ganj Project and enter into a Memorandum of Understanding between Government & HUDCO, until then the status-quo be maintained.

The disposal of Properties at Community Center Andrews Ganj was discussed and finalized without the approval of the Empowered Committee for Andrews Ganj:

The Board further noted the action taken so far for disposal of the guesthouse space and hotel site at HUDCO place, Andrews Ganj. The Board further decided the terms of the Allotment letter to be issued for the HUDCO Place Guesthouses, be finalized jointly by Chairman-cum-Managing Director, HUDCO, Joint Secretary (Finance), and Director Finance, HUDCO. It was decided that detailed rules for disposal of the property be placed before the Board.

HUDCO in the same board meeting in Item No. 2.9 decided regarding the disposal of Hotel Site at HUDCO Place, Andrews Ganj, and setting up of the Screening Committee to scrutinize the bids and take decisions. Etc. The Board considered the proposal and approved the constitution of the following Committee in HUDCO, to screen the offers and take other decisions relating to the disposal of the Hotel Site as under:

Chairman-cum-Managing Director -HUDCO, One Joint Secretary from Ministry of Urban Development - Joint Secretary (EH) Joint Secretary (Finance) Joint Secretary (Urban Development)-, Director Finance-HUDCO-Member, Director Corporate Planning-HUDCO - Member Secretary, Mr. Tar lochan Singh Managing Director, Delhi Tourism & Development Corporation-Member and Mr. R Subramaniam Managing Director, Tourism Finance Corporation, Delhi- Member. Under the recommendations of the Committee, which were duly noted by the Committee of Directors, HUDCO has proceeded with the disposal of guesthouse blocks and Hotel Site at HUDCO Place, Andrews Ganj.

For disposal of Hotel Site, an advertisement was also issued in January 1993 in all leading newspapers in India and abroad, and a brochure has been brought out. The offers for the Guesthouses were also invited from various public sector companies, of which the response has been remote. However, the allotment letters for the guesthouse space to the party who have applied and paid the earnest money are to be issued. The allotment letter has been drafted and contains the terms and conditions of the allotment. The brochure was printed for the Five-Star Hotel Site at HUDCO Place, Andrews Ganj, by advertising for disposal.

BUILDING PLANS

- 5-Star Hotel site
- at HUDCO Place
- Andrews Ganj, New Delhi
- The last date submission offer is 28th February 1993.
- Mr. N. Dharmarajan,
- Project Coordinator (Construction)
- Housing and Urban Development

CORPORATION LIMITED

- (Government of India undertaking)
- HUDCO
- HUDCO House, Lodhi Road, New Delhi

100003: INDIA

- Disposal of a Five-Star Hotel at HUDCO Place
- Developed by HUDCO
- Khelgaon Marg, Andrews Ganj, New Delhi

HOUSING AND URBAN DEVELOPMENT CORPORATION LIMITED

- (Government of India Undertaking)
- Notice Inviting offers for a Five-Star Hotel Site at Community Center being Development by HUDCO
- Near Andrews Ganj, New Delhi.

Under directions from the Government of India Ministry of Urban Development, Housing and Urban Development Corporation Limited proposes to dispose of the following land on leasehold for putting up a hotel not lower than 5 Star.

DESCRIPTION OF LAND:

The hotel site a part of an integrated Urban Community Center complex, being developed on 17.5 acres of the land bounded in North by Andrews Gang Government Quarters, in the south by Sadiq Nagar Government Quarters in West by Khelgaon Marg, and in East by Zonal Green, and Government Quarters Proposed to be developed and constructed shortly. Location of Hotel Site in the Community Center:

A key plan of the location is shown below: Building Controls: The hotel shall be constructed in the building envelope earmarked for the hotel within the parameters of design control of the Urban Design form. Parking spaces and certain common facilities shall be a part of the urban design.

Area: The hotel has been earmarked a buildable space of 25000 sq. meters in an envelope of about 3 acres in the integrated urban design for the Community Center.
Reserve Price: Rs 50 cores for a buildable space of 25000 sq. meters on a building envelope of about 3 acres.

Wasn't it a deceptive scheme, and a trick used to cheat someone by hiding darker secrets because of internal problems behind the closed doors of Government and HUDCO that the land use of the hotel was not permitted in the Community Center at Andrews Ganj as per Master Plan, 1962, but HUDCO and Government used the word earmarked for a hotel?

The light of (1) above, it was decided that keeping in view the terms & conditions of allotment, the memorandum prepared by the HUDCO, draft Memorandum of Understanding should be finalized detailing the background as well as the areas covered so far and the items yet to be accomplished.

After the execution of the Memorandum of Understanding, the HUDCO will be required to furnish a monthly progress report to enable the Government to watch the progress of the conditions spelled out in the MOU.

Accordingly, Chairman-cum-Managing Director, HUDCO was requested to urgently prepare a Memorandum of Understanding for execution between the Government and the HUDCO. After execution of the MOU, the review &

monitoring committee will cease to function, and the HUDCO will take investment & disposal decisions. The meeting ended with a vote of thanks to the Chair.

In pursuance of the decision of the Ministry of Urban Development to wind up the Government Monitoring & Review Committee on Andrews Ganj Project and enter into a Memorandum of Understanding between Government & HUDCO was placed before the board of HUDCO, it was decided that on receipt of these Minutes a reply has been sent to the Ministry indicating that since the execution of the MOU identifying the various issues stated in the Minutes would take some more time; it is hoped the Government Monitoring & Review Committee would continue to function since important policy issues relating to disposal of properties have to be resolved, the Ministry has been informed we shall be shortly sending the Agenda Items and notes or the meeting of the Committee HUDCO succeeded to abolish the Empowered Monitoring Committee for Andrews Ganj project, based on the directions of the Minister of Congress Government through the Secretary of the Ministry of Urban Development, to get the power on the entire Andrews Ganj land. From here, further scams by HUDCO started as independently as a corporation could be, especially under the director corporate who was handling this project. But to act smoothly, I still wrote to the Ministry to continue the Committee until the MOU is decided.

Given the fact, it was a final decision of the ministry that working of the HUDCO is controlled through the Board of Directors, in which joint Secretary of the ministry and Joint Secretary finance from the ministry of finance is the member's disposal policy, and the surplus generated and type of houses to be constructed, the time allowed for construction/handling over, and arrangements for maintenance, etc. have been finalized. The executing agency HUDCO was given the freedom to take investment & policy decisions through or under the authority of its Board of Directors.

It is important to note that the HUDCO board was given all the powers, but at times whenever it suited to ministry, HUDCO's board had no power to decide, and on the other side, after HUDCO's board would decide, then if suited to HUDCO, it was said they needed the approval of the ministry. All were played in as per their conveniences as well as their whims.

Wasn't it a Scam abolishing the Empowered Committee of the Government, which was a precondition of the allotment and all the powers given to HUDCO in respect of Andrews Ganj land?

The Government was worried the investments made by HUDCO in constructing these buildings are being charged @ 17% interest, as agreed by them. Both were worried about the disposal of these properties from 1992 onward itself when various efforts to sell failed. The government had validated the fact of unauthorized constructions, since in between on 1st August 1990, the land use of Andrews Ganj was notified as Convention Center, and the land was to be used for institution purposes. But HUDCO had carried out constructions as per Master Plan, 1962 of the residential buildings constructed on 25-acre land part of the Andrews Ganj land, and the Community Center was being used as per Master Plan, 2001, which was wrong and illegal.

Chapter: Thirty-Two

CMD, HUDCO's Connection with Asian Consolidated Industries Limited

The offers received on the brochure issued by HUDCO were by an Asian Group of hotels only, which were considered by the Screening Committee in the first meeting held on 24th March 1993 for considering the various offers received in response to the advertisement and brochure released to the intending bidders. After the decision of the 1st screening committee meeting, the bids were opened on 24th March 1993.

The details were considered in the 2nd meeting of the screening committee, which was held on 29th March 1993. The offer for a price of Rs. 53.51 crores with a foreign exchange component of Rs 21 crores (42%) manufactured by M/s Asian consolidated Industries Ltd. running Hyatt Regency Hotel in Delhi and other places was found to be acceptable. Since the bidder had raised other issues in the financial terms of the bid. The screening committee considered the details in its 2nd meeting, and their stand to be taken by HUDCO was decided. The Committee authorized Chairman-cum-Managing Director, HUDCO, to have further discussion with the bidder and come up with a specific recommendation to the committee.

Accordingly, Chairman-cum-Managing Director had detailed discussions with the bidder in the light of the decision taken in the 2nd meeting on 8th April 1993, and the bidder has subsequently made available the terms for the offer vide their communication of 27th April 1993. The screening committee considered this communication in its 3rd meeting held on 21st May 1993. The screening committee considered the various issues brought by the bidder, vide his communication dated 27th April 1993. It was decided the bid for Rs. 53.51 crores with Rs. 21 crores foreign exchange component reiterated by the bidder is acceptable, in line with decisions taken in the first meeting.

Regarding various other issues, i.e., relating to increased FAR, increased height as per the provision for increased heights for hotel sites in other areas, and the extent of coverage of the basement outside building line, there are regulations which are looked after by the Delhi Development Authority/Municipal Corporation of Delhi, and the bidder should directly approach them for decision keeping in view the urban design and other statutory controls. The request for allowing the land for utilities as free of cost was not accepted.

Concerning the reduction in the lease rent, it was clarified this would be as decided by the L&DO and as per established norms. Any request for relief is to be made directly by the bidder to L&DO.

About certain general issues relating to the allotment of the guesthouses and shops on the central Plaza, it was clarified these were outside the scope. The disposal work of the Hotel Site and Guesthouses should be taken up separately by the bidder, along with others, when the bids are sought for consideration.

Regarding the payment schedule, the screening committee indicated that the initial payment of 40% will have to be given within one month, and the entire payment is to be given within the schedule of two years. Specific views of the bidder have been sought within a week, along with his final offer for decision.
It is seen that the offer of Rs. 53.51 crores of Asian Consolidated Industries Limited was approved by all the members of the Scrutinizing Committee, but in the end, after meeting the Chairman-cum-Managing Director, HUDCO, Mr. K.K. Bhatnagar, Asian Consolidated Industries Limited withdrew the offer. The reason behind

the withdrawal of the offer was that Mr. K.K. Bhatnagar orally disclosed the fact to Asian Consolidated Industries Limited they have recommended to the Government to change the lease period from 32 years to 99 years, under active consideration.

Mr. K.K. Bhatnagar, Chairman-cum-Managing Director of HUDCO, and Mr. V. Suresh, Director Corporate Planning, were, and Mr. V. Suresh could sense out the disclosure made by Mr. K.K. Bhatnagar. Chairman-cum-Managing Director had also disclosed the fact to the bidder that they may reduce the reserve price if Asian Consolidated Industries Limited would withdraw their offer.

The Joint Secretary, Ministry of Urban Development, Mr. K. Dharmarajan, was made the coordinator who informed on 21, March 1993 to Mr. K. K. Bhatnagar Chairman & Managing Director HUDCO that kindly recalled the discussions we had along with the Additional Secretary on the subject of the implementation of the integrated project at Andrews Gang. Keeping in view the various issues related to the implementation of the project, the works are so far done by the Monitoring and Review Committee of the Ministry of Urban Development, the clear role of

HUDCO regarding decisions now for disposal and investment-related issues. All the three earlier communications sent from the Ministry vide letter of 1st November 1990, June 1992 and December 1992 have been amalgamated.

A new letter would now be issued. I am enclosing a copy of the same for your perusal. I hope this will keep in view all the issues discussed jointly between the Ministry of Urban Development and HUDCO.

Land & Development Officer amended the terms of allotment of Andrews Ganj land to HUDCO on 2nd April 1993[5], amending them as approved by the Ministry of Urban Development, in which the condition for using Andrews Ganj remained the same, and the condition for the approval of construction plans remained unchanged. The condition of land use of Community Center and the construction plans were:

The land for the Community Center should be utilized for the development of Hostel and guesthouse facilities, conference hall, shopping & other Community Center

[5] (HOUSING AND URBAN DEVELOPEMENT CORPORATION LIMITED, 2012)

facilities, as per the Urban Design for the complex approved by the Ministry of Urban Development.

The local body shall approve the construction plans and Delhi Development Authority, Delhi Urban Art Commission, and the L&DO before undertaking any construction on the land.

Isn't it that, despite the stipulations that the hotel could not be constructed in the Community Center, and that the construction plans were to be approved before undertaking any construction on the land, HUDCO completely violated these terms, leading to the Andrews Ganj land Scam attempting to commit fraud?

Chapter: Thirty-Three

Lease Period in Fresh Allotment to Land & Development Office Changed from 32 Years to 99 Years by Government

HUDCO had fixed the reserve price of the 5-Star hotel for Rs. 50 crores plus the cost of common facilities, but failed to receive any bids in February 1993, and the offer of Rs. 53.51 crores made by Asian Consolidated Industries Limited had been withdrawn for the reasons best known to the boss of the Scrutinizing Committee.

HUDCO placed the difficulties before its board being faced in the disposal of the properties in the Community Center at Andrews Ganj, due to which HUDCO in its board meeting reduced the reserve price of the hotel land to Rs. 39 Crores, which was approved. HUDCO was unable to dispose of the Guesthouses, except one allotment of one guesthouse was issued in January 1993.

The Under Secretary, Ministry of Urban Development, Mr. B.R. Dhiman issued an allotment letter dated 15th June 1993 to the Land & Development officer regarding allotment of land to the Housing & Urban Development Corporation Ltd. At Pinjrapole (Andrews Ganj)

In supersession of all earlier letters dated 1st November 1990, 10th June 1992, and 28th December 1992 issued on the above subject, I am directed to convey the sanction of the president to the allotment of land measuring about 42.6 acres at Pinjrapole, Andrews Ganj, as per plan in favor of HUDCO as per terms and conditions:

17.6 acres of land for the Community Center will be leased on payment of a token premium of re.1 and annual ground rent of re.1 per acre for 99 years. The land for the Community Center should be utilized for the development of hostel and guesthouse facilities, conference hall, shopping, and other Community Center facilities, as per the urban design for the complex approved by this ministry. HUDCO shall take all investment decisions for the whole project, and disposal decisions for the properties in the Community Center.

The Government will finalize the details of the sub-leasing arrangements in respect of facilities development on the Community Center land, in consultation with HUDCO. A memorandum of Understanding shall be executed between the Ministry of Urban Development and HUDCO, detailing the terms and conditions for the execution of the project. This issues with the concurrence of the Finance Division vide their U.O. No.1418/Joint Secretary/93 dated 3rd June 1993.

In my view as an author, it is curious that the Ministry bypassed all the rules, laws in changing the lease period, but the Land & Development Officer declined to issue the allotment letter of 99 years to HUDCO and declined to amend the terms being an honest officer as compared with the Joint Secretary (Land) and Joint Secretary (Finance).

Although 32 years lease period to 99 years of allotment to Land & Development Officer by the Ministry to HUDCO was changed on 15th June 1993 by issuing a fresh allotment letter to the Land & Development Office, Land & Development Officer did not issue any allotment to HUDCO for 99 years until 19th March 1996, nor HUDCO paid the lease fee, and neither HUDCO accepted the terms even after 19th March 1996.

It is on record the lease period of 32 years was not changed by the Land & Development Officer, but HUDCO went on to sell the properties without any proper allotment in their favor, without even accepting the allotment terms of 32 years, and without paying Rs. 75/- as lease fee since the land was at the cost of Re. 1/- per acre, even if the lease period is from 32 years to 99 years.

The lease period was decided to be changed by the Government from 32 years lease to 99 years at the same lease price at Re. 1/= per acre, but HUDCO decided to reduce the reserve price to Rs. 39 crores for inviting subsequent bids, which was orally indicated by Mr. K.K. Bhatnagar to Asian Consolidated Industries Limited. Now it was sure for Asian Consolidated to get the land for a 99-year lease at Rs. 40 Crores, as there had been no bidders other than them.

HUDCO in the 183rd Board meeting held on 9th July 1993 with the members present Mr. K.K. Bhatnagar–Chairman-cum-Managing Director, HUDCO, Mr. V. Suresh–Director Corporate Planning, HUDCO, Mr. SS favor–Director, Mr. GS Bhandari–Director, Mr. RMS Liberhan–Executive Director (Vigilance) (As special invitee), Mr. Gopal Krishan–Company Secretary, the disposal of the Guesthouses at Andrews Ganj was finalized, and the disposal of the hotel site was finalized based on the decision of the Ministry of Urban Development

In pursuance of the decision in the 177th board meeting, the matter was taken up with the Ministry of Urban Development through detailed discussions with the

Secretary, Urban Development, and other key officers of the Ministry regarding the methodology to be adopted for implementation, and the effective monitoring systems in respect of Andrews Ganj project. It was noted that as per allotment dated 15th June 1993 to the Land & Development Office by the Government, has been changed from 32 years to 99 years, and now all investment decisions for the projects and disposal decisions for the property in the Community Center were to be taken by HUDCO.
The Board further noted the action taken so far for disposal of the guesthouse space and hotel site at HUDCO place, Andrews Ganj. The Board further decided the terms of the allotment letter to be issued. It was decided that detailed rules for disposal of the property be placed before the Board.

In the light of the notice giving a brief of the subject matter and related provision in the proposal being submitted for consideration of the cabinet regarding land as a resource for stepping up investment in the construction of the general pool accommodation, after detailed deliberation on the subject matter, it was believed.

Since working of the HUDCO is controlled through the Board of Directors, in which Joint Secretary (HD) & Joint Secretary (Finance) are members, the need for having a review & monitoring committee for the Pinjrapole project was reviewed, and it was thought once a memorandum of understanding detailing terms & conditions for execution of the project, its disposal policy, and the surplus generated and type of houses to be constructed, the time allowed for construction/handing over, and arrangements for maintenance, etc. The executing agency should have the freedom to take investment & policy decisions through or under the authority of its Board of Directors.

Isn't it a scam that CMD, HUDCO did not accept the offer of Rs? 53.51 crores of Asian Consolidated Industries Limited for 32 years lease against a reserve price of Rs? 50 crores of 5-Star Hotel land at Andrews Ganj, instead CMD through board reduced the reserve price to Rs. 39 crores for 99 years?

Chapter: Thirty-Four

HUDCO's Justification of Rs. 39 Crores Reserve Price for Hotel Land Earmarked in Community Center

HUDCO in his board meeting no. 183.4.10 regarding disposal of hotel site at Andrews Gang referred to the decision regarding disposal of hotel site at Andrews Ganj, which was considered by HUDCO's Board in its 182nd meeting (Item No.182.4.4) that subsequently, the screening committee in its 4th meeting held on 10th June 1993 had decided on the various issues related to stages of payments. Issues related to permission for taking up the service component by the hotelier and acquiring the built car parking space in the basement at a predetermined price, the changed payment pattern in Indian currency and Foreign Exchange, etc.

M/s Asian Consolidated industries ltd. In their communication dated 29th June 1993 and 7th July 1993, they indicated their inability to keep up their earlier commitment for foreign exchange contribution, participation of the international collaboration in the hotel project, without the tie-up for disposal of the shopping complex-cum-department store in the central plaza. The screening committee, in its 5th meeting held on 8th July 1993, has informed Asian consolidated industries ltd and invites revised price bids. The Committee has also started a review of the Reserve price of Rs. 39 crores earlier decided upon for enlisting increased participation through bids from the hotel industry could be done.

The board of directors of HUDCO was informed in its 183rd meeting that the Screening Committee, which was appointed to screen the bids relating to disposal of the hotel site, rejected the bid-offer of M/s Asian consolidated industries ltd and recommended inviting fresh price bids. They have also recommended a revision of the reserve price downwards.

Accordingly, the revised reserve price has been worked out at Rs. 39 crores. It is, however, perceived that even at a reduced reserve price, it may be difficult to get an acceptable offer. Hence, it is proposed the screening committee may be empowered to consider a bid at a maximum of 15% lower than the revised reserve price of Rs. 39 crores, the details of fixation of reserve price for a hotel site and cultural center, comparison of sale value viz-a-viz cost (provisional), details of cost calculation for various sites at Andrews Ganj, and the draft advertisement for the hotel site was placed before the board.

The board may kindly approve the revise of the reserve price of Rs. 39 crores, with the power to the screening committee to consider any bid below a maximum of 15% of the reserve price, and the revised terms and conditions for disposal of the hotel site. It is proposed to seek the approval of the Ministry of Urban Development to these proposals since this would involve changes in the reserve price and procedure already approved by them.
Fixation of reserve price for hotel site at Andrews Gang was justified as follows:

HUDCO had a fixed reserve price of Rs. 50 crores for the land cost of 25000 sq meters. Built-up special based on the following assumptions: -

1. Notified commercial rate: Rs.23,200 per Sq. Mt. (for FAR 150)
2. The rate for 100 FAR: Rs 15,466 per sq Mt.
3. Add 20 percent for the: Rs.03,094 per sq mt.

Notified commercial rate

4. Total cost per Se. Mt.: Rs.18,560.00
5. Land cost Rs 18560x25000: Rs. 46.40 crores (Sq. m)
6. Add 10% HUDCO Profit: Rs. 04364 crores

Total: - Rs. 51.04 crores

The reserve price was accordingly fixed at Rs 50 crores plus the cost of common facilities, which was estimated at around Rs. 15 crores.

Based on this reserve price, HUDCO invited offers through newspaper advertisement twice, and only two offers were received, i.e. (i) Asian consolidated industries limited quoted Rs. 53.51 crores and (ii) M/s Asian hotel limited quoted Rs 30 crores. M/s Asian consolidated industries ltd who quoted a price of Rs. 53.51 crores have withdrawn their offer, as decided by the screening committee in its meeting held on 8th July 1993, the reserve price has been reworked out as per the following details: -

The notified commercial rate for Andrews Gang: Rs 23,200 per sq mt. (for (F) AR 150) from 1st April 1991 to March 1994

The rate for 100 FAR: Rs. 15,466 per sq Mt.

Area of hotel site (built-up space): Rs 25000 sq mt

Total cost (@ Rs. 15466 per: Rs 38.665 crores

Smut)

Or say: Rs (valid up to 31st March 1994)

NOTE: - 20 percent increase over the notified area, and 10 percent profit margin has not been included, as the same forms part of the notified commercial rate valid until 31st March 1994. The reserve price shall, however, have to be revised in case 31st March does not dispose of the hotel site 1994.

Comparison of Sale Value vis-à-vis Cost (Provisional) (Rs in lakhs)

- Estimated Receipts Hotel site 3,900.00
- Guesthouses5,800.00
- Cultural center plot 200.00
    - Shops in guesthouse Estimated 1,100.00
    - Shopping arched Reserve 2,500.00
    - Shopping Mall Price not 2,200.00
    - Offices Yet decided 1,000.00,
    - Cost of common services

Recoverable from hotel site 18,350.00

- Estimated Expenditure
- The Guesthouses 9,628.87
- Zonal Green 116.73 ----- 9,745.60, Or say 9,750.00
- Estimated surplus
- Utilization of surplus
- Residential houses 6,343.62

- Contingencies (on entire cost) 804.46 7,148.08

Net estimated surplus Based on the average tentative price of Rs. 15.00 lakhs per room, as indicated in the brochure.

It was observed in the board meeting that on behalf of the Ministry of Urban Development. HUDCO is developing the Integrated Complex–HUDCO Place at Andrews Gang at Khelgaon Marg. This complex has guesthouse accommodation in two clusters. Cluster-A & Cluster-B. Each cluster has six blocks. Thus, there are 12 blocks with an average of 40 numbers of rooms in each block. The total number of rooms is around 480, which are located on 1st, 2nd, 3rd floors. The ground floor has specialty restaurants, discerning shopping, and other amenities and facilities like a health club, swimming pool, centralized air conditioning, hot water supply, and also a co-terminus with 18 acres Zonal Green.

A brochure indicating the salient features of Guesthouses was prepared by HUDCO, and Chairman-cum-Managing Director, HUDCO to the following agencies sent copies with a request to send their offer for purchasing the Guesthouses:

- Central Public Sector undertaking - 190 numbers
- Chief Secretaries of State Government/Union Territories and Resident Representatives of the State and Union Territories - 42 numbers
- Central Government Ministries - 6 numbers

Subsequently, letters were also sent to Chief Executives of Banks/All India Financial Institutions/Insurance Companies by Mr. K. J Reddy, Secretary, Ministry of Urban Development. Based on the above response so far received from the Government Organization/Agenda were the Government of Karnataka–1 block, Punjab State Industrial Development Corporation–1 block, Indian Oil Corporation–1 block, Government of Haryana–1 block, Neyveli Lignite Corporation–1 block.

Indian Farmers Fertilizer Cooperative Limited (IFFCO) has indicated its desire to purchase one block and their firm offer after their board meeting is awaited. Since the response from the Government Organization was not satisfactory, it was decided to invite a few corporate industrial houses, e.g., Tesco, Reliance Industries, Lane Toubro, etc. The brochure of Guesthouses has already been sent to the 21 largest business houses by way of intimation.

The response from these organizations has been limited, and only two organizations, viz Tisco and ITC Ltd., have informed HUDCO that representatives will be in touch with HUDCO shortly.

Given the above position, it is proposed to offer the balance guesthouse to the private sector, mainly corporate industrial houses and guesthouse groups. The offer is proposed to be invited from these agencies by bringing out suitable advertisement press. The reserve price for the rooms shall be Rs. 15 lacs per room of 1 bay width. It must be for a minimum of one floor. The preference to be given an acceptable offer of whole block price bids would be invited within a specific period with two whole blocks containing agency background, the other containing price bid. The terms of payment are in three installments.

- 40% within 1 month of allotment
- 40% within 3 months of allotment
- 20% at the time of giving possession

Delayed payment beyond the period will incur 18% penal interest.

HUDCO went on to sell the properties without the approval of the layout plan or the sanction of building plans. The ministry officials as well as HUDCO officers knew that the buildings were illegal and that as per Master Plan 1962, the land use of the hotel was not permitted. But in any case, such a scam was by the Government or by HUDCO, which was acceptable and could not yet be treated as a scam.

My dear readers, my view is, it is an open scam by HUDCO since the reduction in the reserve price from Rs. 50 crores to Rs. 39 crores, with an increase in lease period from 32 years to 99 years

Chapter: Thirty-Five

HUDCO's Attempt to Sell the Five-Star Hotel Land

HUDCO in its board meeting No. 184.2.4. Finalized the disposal of the Hotel Site and the advertisement for selling hotel land, keeping a reserve price of Rs. 39 crores, as approved in the last meeting. The board recorded the minutes:

The board of directors of HUDCO was informed in its 183rd meeting that the screening committee, which was appointed to screen the bids relating to disposal of the hotel site, rejected the bid-offer of M/S Asian Consolidated Industries Ltd and recommended inviting fresh price bids. They have also recommended a revision of the reserved price downwards.

Accordingly, the revised Reserve price has been worked out at Rs. 39 crores. It is, however, felt that even at a reduced reserve price, it may be difficult to get an acceptable offer. Hence, it is proposed it may empower the screening committee to consider a bid at a maximum 15% lower than the revised Reserve price of Rs. 39 crores. The details of fixation of the Reserve price for a hotel site and cultural Centre, Comparison of sale value viz-a-viz cost (provisional), details of cost calculation for various sites at

Andrews Ganj, and the draft advertisement for Hotel Site are also placed.

The board may kindly approve the revised Reserve price of Rs. 39 Crores, with power to the Screening Committee to consider any bid below a maximum of 15% of the reserve price, and the revised terms and conditions for disposal of the hotel site. It is proposed to seek the approval of the Ministry of Urban Development to these proposals since this would involve changes in the reserve price and procedure already approved by them.

The board considered the proposal and approved the revised reserve price at Rs 35.00 Crores. The Board further decided to approve the revised terms and conditions for disposal of the hotel site. The Board also decided that, because these involve a change in the reserve price and procedure already approved by the Ministry of Urban Development, the approval of the Ministry to these revised proposals be obtained. The notice inviting offers was circulated and offers were called for 5-Star Hotel land.

- Housing and Urban Development Corporation Limited

- (Government of India Undertaking)
- Notice Inviting of Offers for A Five-Star Hotel Site at Comm Centre Being Development by HUDCO Near Andrews Ganj Delhi

Under directors from the Government of India, Ministry of Urban Development, Housing Urban Development Corporation Limited proposes to dispose of the following on leasehold for putting up a hotel with a rating not lower than 5 Star:

Description of land: The hotel site a part of an integrated Urban Community Center complex, being developed on 17.5 acres of the land bounded in North by Andrews Gang Government Quarters, in the south by Sadiq Nagar Government Quarters in West by Khelgaon Marg, and in East by Zonal Green, and Government Quarters Proposed to be developed and constructed shortly.

Location of Hotel site the Community Center: Development on 17.5 acres of the land bounded in the north by Andrews Gang Government Quarters, in the south by Sadiq Nagar Government Quarters by Khelgaon Marg, and in the east by Zonal green, and Government proposed to be developed and constructed show: -

Building Controls: The hotels shall be constructed in the building envelope earmarked for the Hotel within the parameters of the Design Control of the Urban Design Form parking spaces, and certain common facilities shall be a part of the Urban Design.

Area: The hotel has been earmarked a buildable space of 25000 sq. meters. In an envelope of about 3 acres in the integrated Urban Design for the Community Center. The present permissible height as prescribed by the competent authority is 36 m. However, any relaxation in height restriction beyond the prescribed limit would be as per the decision of the statutory authority. If the statutory authorities approve additional build-up area FAR for the additional space over and above 25000 sq. Mt. Premium will be charged Rs 10,000/- per additional sq. mt. of space permitted.

Common Facilities: The urban design provides for common facilities in the Central Plaza of the Community Center to be shared by all categories of users, including hotels, guesthouses, shops, offices, and cultural centers. The cost of these facilities, including building, equipment, and ancillaries. All users shall share costs in proportion to their use of these facilities. The facilities include an underground parking plant room, water tank, HVAC, Electric Substation, DG Sets Boilers, External Serves, Pumps Steam Piping, Scrubber, etc. It is proposed to discuss this issue with the eligible bidders to explain the concept and sharing of costs and the maintenance of the common facilities.

Reserve Price: Rs. 39 crores for a buildable space of 25000 sq. mt. on a building envelope of about 3 acres.

Cost of common facilities: The approximate proportionate cost of the common facilities to be shared by the Hotel is about Rs 16.50 crores. This will, however, be subject to change as per the actual cost when the work is completed. Alternatively, the bidders may be offered space to enable them to install and maintain their utilities. In that case, only the cost of about 400 sq. mt. of space at the rate of Rs. 15466 per sq. Mt. (FAR 100) will be charged. The bidder may also have the option to provide their utilities in their own allotted space. In that case, no additional cost will be charged. The portion of car parking space for 418 cars in the central basement will be allotted to the Hotel use at Rs

6.70 crores approximately to cover the proportionate cost of construction.

The offers shall be submitted to the Director (Corporate Planning), HUDCO, HUDCO House, Lodhi Road, New Delhi-110003 to reach him on or before the offer received after this date shall be returned unopened / shall not be considered.

The reduced reserve price of Rs. 35 crores were objected by the director of Corporate Planning, Mr. V. Suresh, as he was aware of the connection of Mr. K. K. Bhatnagar Chairman-cum-Managing Director HUDCO with Asian Hotels Group. Due to his objections, the approval was sent to the Ministry.

The reduction of the reserve price of hotel land for Rs. 35.00 crores and the increase of the lease period from 32 years to 99 years resulted in a Scam by HUDCO. HUDCO continued to try to dispose of Guesthouse blocks and the hotel land without disclosing the illegal construction and non-approval of the layout plan. Even Delhi Urban Art Commission observed the conceptual approval does not mean the final approval, and the building has been constructed without the final approval of the layout plan and warned the Architect for such wrongdoings. Delhi Urban Art Commission also confirmed the same to the Municipal Corporation of Delhi.

The statement made by the Architect was again false that he had submitted the plans as per the old Master Plan when on the record the fact is the plans were submitted as per the new Master Plan, rather even the construction was carried out as per the new master plan by HUDCO, and Municipal Corporation of Delhi categorically objected to the same. Delhi Urban Art Commission approved the layout plan under the pressure of the Ministry of Urban Development. Still, Delhi Urban Art Commission informed the Municipal Corporation of Delhi that the approval is subject to strictly if the drawings are as per Master Plan, Zonal Plan, building bye-laws, Fire Fighting Regulations and Policy instructions of the Government of India, which the Municipal Corporation of Delhi should strictly check and follow. Delhi Urban Art Commission in its 749th meeting held on Friday, 27th August 1993 with the members present Mr. Mir Nasrullah- Chairman, Mr. R. Bannerji–Member, Mr. M.T. Meshram Secretary, Mr. Vinod Kumar- Assistant Secretary (tech.) and Advisors: Mr. A. P Kanvinde, Mr.

Jasbir Sachdev, Mr. Ajoy Chowdhury, Mr. Ravindra Bhan, Mr. Sharat Das in item 8 considered the Layout plan of the Community Center at Pinjrapole, Andrews Ganj, and the minutes were minuted:

The proposal had been received through Town Planner, Municipal Corporation of Delhi, for Commissions for final approval of layout plan. Earlier, the scheme was approved twice at the conceptual stage of the commission's meeting. Most of the buildings which are approved at the conceptual stage have already been built. A conceptual approval does not mean the formal approval of the commission. The commission introduced for the project this method when these used to be forwarded by the local bodies.

Formal approval of the commission is necessary before building activities could be started, and before building activities could be started. Architect, Mr. Jasbir Sawhney, explained that he had submitted the plans to the Municipal Corporation of Delhi after getting the conceptual approval from the commission, and these plans have been formulated as per the norms of the old master plan. Meanwhile, due to the change of Master Plan, the Municipal Corporation of Delhi was reluctant to approve the layout plan of the project. The promoters obtained the approval of exception from the Government, which took considerable time. Since the Promoter was assured, the relaxation will be given to them to save time, they started the execution of the project.

The commission reluctantly accepted the explanation simply because the project is well-conceived and approved the proposal. So far as some parts of the project which are yet to be started are concerned with the approval of the promoters, and the architects will not take the commission's approval for granted.

The Secretary of, Delhi Urban Art Commission, Mr. M.T. Meshram on 8th September 1993 informed The Town Planner, Municipal Corporation of Delhi, Town Hall regarding the Layout Plan of Community Center at Pinjrapole, Andrews Gang.

The above project forwarded vide your letter no. 1/25/9C/TT/Municipal Corporation of Delhi/676/92 dated 25th June 1993 on receipt of a proposal, etc. vide architect's letter no. Nil dated 30th July 1993 was considered in its meeting of 27th August 1993, and the following observations were made: -

The above-mentioned proposal had been received through the town planner. Municipal Corporation of Delhi for Commission's final approval of layout plan. Earlier, the scheme was approved twice at the conceptual stage of the Commission's meeting.

The scheme was examined and discussed with the Architects, and the Commission observed that:
Most of the buildings which were approved at the conceptual stage have already been built. A conceptual approval does not mean to be formal approval of the Commission. The Commission introduced this method to reduce delays in approving the project by the Commission when they would be forwarded by the local bodies.

Formal approval of the Commission is necessary before building activities are started. Architect Mr. Jasbir Sawhney explained he had submitted the plans to the Municipal Corporation of Delhi after getting the conceptual approval from the Commission, and their plans have been formulated as per the norms of the old Master Plan.

Meanwhile, due to the change of the Master Plan, the Municipal Corporation of Delhi was reluctant to approve the Layout Plan of the project. The promoters obtained the approval of exception from the Government, which has taken considerable time. Since the promoter was assured, the relaxation would be given to them to save time, they started the execution of the project.

The Commission reluctantly accepted the explanation, because the project is well-conceived and approved the proposal. So far as other parts of the project which are yet to be started are concerned, the approval of the commission is mandatory, and it is hoped the promoters and the architect will not take the commission's approval for granted.

In view of the above, strictly subject to the conditions mentioned above, a set of approved drawings in respect of the layout plan only for further necessary action if the same is otherwise as Master plan, zonal plan, building bylaws, firefighting regulators, and policy instructions of the Government of India.

Isn't it a scam to sell land for use by the Government through HUDCO, the Government Company, without disclosing that the land use is not yet regularized and that the layout plans are still not approved even at the conceptual stage?

Isn't it a scam that the Government builds unauthorized buildings without following any building bylaws, and then attempts to sell without the disclosures, when even the Delhi Urban Art Commission observed while approving conceptual stage layout that most of the buildings have been completed without approvals?

Chapter: Thirty-Six

HUDCO's Advertisement to Sell All Properties at Community Center at Andrews Ganj

HUDCO in its 188th board meeting held on 25th November 1993 regarding the hotel site and Guesthouses in which the members present Mr. K.K. Bhatnagar–Chairman-cum-Managing Director, HUDCO, Mr. V. Suresh – Director Corporate Planning HUDCO, Mr. S S Meenakshisundram, Director, Mr. AP Sinha–Director, Mr. RMS Liberhan–Executive Director (Vigilance) (As special invitee), Mr. Gopal Krishan–Company Secretary finalized the disposal of Guesthouses in HUDCO Place–The board while approving the proposal contained in board note, also authorized Chairman-cum-Managing Director to consider proposals that may be received for the disposal of Guesthouses. The board also felt that expeditious action for disposal of the Guesthouses could be taken to ensure an inflow of resources for implementing the integrated project.

Disposal of Cultural & Art Centre site of HUDCO Place Andrews Gang, New Delhi–The Board, after consideration, approved the action to be taken as proposed in the agenda note and decided that HUDCO should not take up the construction as proposed in the last paragraph of the agenda note.

Accordingly, press advertisement was given in the following newspapers:

- Hindustan Times, Time of India, Hindu, Statesman, Hindu International.

A brochure was prepared, giving all the details, terms and conditions, etc., for the disposal of Guesthouses. The last date for submitting a sealed tender bid was 1st November 1993. However, until the stipulated time, no offer from any organizations was received. Hence, as of date, the following organizations have bought Guesthouses:

- Government of Karnataka–1 block, Indian Oil Corporation–1 block, Government of Haryana–1 Block, Neyveli Lignite Corporation–1 Block.
- Earlier, Punjab State Industrial Development Corporation had offered to buy 1 floor, and they had deposited the earnest money of Rs. 9.75 lacs. However, later on, they changed their mind and requested the return of the earnest money which has since been returned to them.

It is now proposed to again make vigorous efforts to sell the Guesthouses to the Public Sector/State Government/Central Government/Financial

Institution/Private Section Guesthouse Group at the price of Rs. 37,690/- per sq. Meters, which is the rate at which 2 blocks and 2 floors were sold to four parties mentioned in paragraph 3 above. It is also proposed to call some leading private corporate houses who had purchased the brochure for a discussion. The possibility of combined disposal of hotel site/commercial complex/Guesthouses is also being looked into. Disposal of Cultural and Art Centre site at HUDCO Place, Andrews Ganj, New Delhi

The board of directors of HUDCO, in its 184th meeting, had approved the proposal to dispose of the Cultural and Art center at HUDCO Place, Andrews Gang, New Delhi to public organizations, trusts, registered societies engaged in cultural activities or proposing to promote cultural activities and corporate business houses. The reserve price was fixed at Rs. 2 crores plus the proportionate cost of common facilities, which worked out to approximately Rs. 1.50 crores.

Accordingly, a brochure was prepared to mention all salient features, reserve price, proportionate cost of common services, and mode of payment, etc. It was advertised in the following newspapers:

- Hindustan times-New Delhi, Time of India - New Delhi & Mumbai, Hindu-Madras, Statement-Calcutta, Hindu International.

The last date for receiving the offer was 22nd November 1993. However, until the last date, no offer was received from any prospective buyers.

It is now proposed again to take the following action on the disposal of the Cultural site:

Contact big corporate houses/societies and public organizations/cultural bodies, and call them for discussions and offer them the plot at the reserve price of Rs. 2 crores plus the proportionate cost of common services.

Attempt to dispose of the Cultural Site along with the Guesthouses and/or hotel site/shopping arcade and the mall as one complete package.

Chairman-cum-Managing Director may be empowered to make changes to the payment schedule depending on the discussions with the perspective.

If through the above modes, it is impossible to dispose of the Cultural site, then HUDCO may construct the Cultural Centre itself to enhance the build its corporate image.

Mr. R. K Sharma, Project Coordinator, Asian Consolidated Industries Limited, submitted a letter dated 29th December 1993 to Mr. K.K. Bhatnagar Chairman-cum-Managing Director, HUDCO, confirming the meeting again with the Chairman-cum-Managing Director to meet with you again. I would like to reiterate that the Asian Group is committed to setting up a deluxe hotel in New Delhi. Indeed, we are looking to HUDCO to help us in realizing the project envisaged by us. It would indeed be a unique project, if the Hotel, Retail, and Guesthouse could be combined as a mixed-use facility.

During the past few months, we have extensively studied the international market and visited several such mixed-use facilities primarily in the United States. We have also met several international consultants, developers, master planners, and architects who specialize in such mixed-use facilities. It will be our pleasure to share our findings with you. We can give a presentation to you and your colleagues at your convenience.

We have also received the approval of the foreign investment promotion board (FIPB) for the development of the mixed-use facility. A copy of the same has already been given to you for your information.

We are eager to hear from you about the refloating of the tender for the Hotel and retail sites. We would be quick on development the same, along with the Guesthouses. We can also submit a proposal to set up leisure and entertainment facilities in the open areas, in the center of the complex. Isn't it a Scam that HUDCO CMD had proximity to the Officer of Asian Consolidated Industries Limited to leak all the information orally in the meetings held?

Chapter: Thirty-Seven

HUDCO CMD Mr. K.K. Bhatnagar Vs Mr. V. Suresh Director Corporate Planning

As Mr. V. Suresh, Director, Corporate Planning of HUDCO, was against the Chairman, HUDCO favoring Asian Hotel group. Before the proposed brochures for the reserve price of Rs. 35 crores came out, Mr. V. Suresh wanted to sabotage the understanding of Mr. K. K. Bhatnagar, Chairman-cum-Managing Director, HUDCO with Asian Hotels. He spoke in the last week of January 1994 to one of the Executive Directors of MS Shoes East Ltd., whose Managing Director was Mr. Pavan Sachdeva. Mr. V. Suresh, who was known to Mr. G.K. Iyer, Executive Director of MS Shoes East Limited, told him to get the offer from the company for the 5-Star Hotel Land for Rs. 50 crores, although the approved reserve price was Rs. 35 crores.

Mr. G. K. Iyer, in a meeting of the company MS Shoes East Ltd., which was already foraying into the hotels, submitted the proposal of Mr. V. Suresh that this land can be taken for Rs. 50 crores and an offer be sent to HUDCO. The Chairman-cum-Managing Director of MS Shoes East Ltd. approved the suggestion of Mr. G.K. Iyer with a commitment that if this offer of Rs. 50 Crores is accepted, something would be done for V. Suresh. Pavan Sachdeva directed one of his consultants, Mr. Rajan, to prepare a letter along with the check which will be sent to HUDCO under the signatures of MS Shoes Chairman-cum-Managing Director.

One of the consultants of MS Shoes was friendly with a few other companies, and was chatty, and could not control to leak out the confidential information of MS Shoes. Before MS Shoes could send any such offer to HUDCO, due to a leak of information by the consultant, Mr. Rajan, to Mr. Kalsi of Phoenix Shoes to send such offers to HUDCO.

An offer was sent on 18th February 1994 by Phoenix Shoes from their company, Phoenix Overseas Ltd., for the purchase of the Andrews Ganj properties, more particularly the 5-Star Hotel Land, for Rs. 50 crores, by sending a check. The offer was sent before the offer was sent by MS Shoes. The representatives of Phoenix Shoes met Chairman-cum-Managing Director of HUDCO in respect of Andrews Ganj project and sent the offer on 4th March 1994 for all the properties at Andrews Ganj through one of his companies, Phoenix Overseas Ltd. Under the signatures of its General Manager, Mr. Harinder Singh, to the

Chairman-cum-Managing Director, HUDCO, regarding the purchase of properties at Andrews Gang.

The letter dated 4th March 1994 of Phoenix Overseas Ltd. More specifically, stated:1. This refers to our letter dated 18th February 1994 and subsequent meeting with you on the purchase of properties. 2. We are now looking for a bigger share in the property and are keen to purchase the same as a package that constitutes as follows: a. 3 acres of land earmarked for the hotel. b. 9000 sq. meters of land for building shopping complexes. c. 2500 sq. meters of land earmarked for cultural projects. d. The entire cluster of 6 in number Guesthouse Bleach facing the Hotel site. 3. We, therefore, request you to let us know the combined price of all the properties for us to negotiate and finalize the deal.

MS Shoes through its Chairman-cum-Managing Director, Mr. Pavan Sachdeva, submitted to HUDCO on 21st March 1994 & 23rd March 1994 for purchase of properties at Andrews Ganj through MS Shoes and another company MS World Links Hotel Ltd. The offer: we are a part of the MS group of which MS Shoes East Ltd. Is the flagship company. Our group’s net worth is Rs. 200 crores as of date. MS Group of companies is headed by Mr. Pavan

Sachdeva, a young and dynamic industrialist. The group is growth-oriented and professionally managed, with a total export turnover of Rs.300 crores. Our group is currently implementing several projects with financial assistance from IDBI/IFCI, including Indian-made Foreign Liquor (IMFL) in the assisted sector with Haryana State Industrial Development Corporation Ltd. and Horticulture project.

In MS World link Hotels Ltd, we are planning to set up modern 5-star Hotels in Udaipur, Jodhpur, and Goa in collaboration with a leading hotel chain, which will provide their technical and managerial hotel expertise in managing these hotels. We are also proposing to set up a 5-Star Hotel in Calcutta/Bombay. Besides, we are also bidding for the wildflower hall in Shimla, which will be re-built into a 5-Star Hotel. Discussions are in the final stage with the HP Government in this regard. Here also, the chain of hotels would be associated with the management and said hotel chain can be furnished to you upon allotment of the sites sought by us from HUDCO.

We are informed HUDCO has constructed Guesthouses with star facilities in Khel Gaon Marg, Andrews Ganj, New Delhi. We understand there are 9 blocks available in clusters 'A' and 'B', while we would be interested in the allotment of all 9 blocks of Guesthouses with star facilities. Should that not be possible, we would request you to kindly consider the allotment of at least all 6 blocks in cluster 'B', for which earnest money of Rs. 210 lakhs only vide check no. 586780 and 586781 drawn on Canara bank. If the balance 3 blocks in cluster 'A' are also agreed to be allotted to us, we shall immediately deposit the earnest money for the same.

In order that we may develop the entire complex as a top-of-the-class Guesthouse-cum-shopping plaza in the capital, we shall be glad if the restaurants, as well as shopping areas located on the ground floor of each block, are simultaneously allotted to us at the price to be fixed by HUDCO. A check for Rs. 75 lacs only towards approximate earnest money on this account for all 6 blocks in cluster 'B'. The blocks are proposed to be allotted to us together. We appreciate it much if a discount of up to 10 is granted to us on the value fixed by HUDCO for all the six or nine blocks whatsoever may be.

We are informed that HUDCO proposed to dispose of a Cultural Centre site in HUDCO Place, Khel Gaon Marg,

Andrews Ganj, New Delhi for Rs. 2 crores. As we propose to develop and project the entire complex as a top-class Guesthouse-cum-shopping Centre, besides building a grand 5 Star luxury hotel, we would also request you to kindly allot the cultural Centre to us. This would be an added attraction to the visitors, who can witness elegant, enlightened, and sophisticated cultural shows, and are programmed to be held at the proposed Cultural Centre regularly.

We are enclosing a check for Rs.1 lakh only towards earnest money for the Cultural Centre. We are enclosing our latest audited balance sheet for the year ended March 31, 1993, along with provisional unaudited financial results for the period ended December 31, 1993.

Besides, we understand HUDCO intends to dispose of the 5-Star Hotel site at HUDCO Place, Khel Gaon Marg, Andrews Ganj, New Delhi. We shall be glad if the site is allotted to us at the reserve price of Rs. 50 crores for a buildable space of 25000 sq. meters on a building envelope of about 3 acres. Although earnest money of Rs. 1 lac only is required to be deposited, as an indication of our seriousness, we are sending herewith a check for Rs. 50 lacs only in your favor, along with our offer.

Our endeavor will not only be to enhance the image and prestige of HUDCO by developing this grand Plaza, but also provide the people with products and services under one roof and day-to-day running by the well-experienced five-Star Hotel Chain company in India.

Municipal Corporation of Delhi considered the revised layout plan for General Pool Housing on 12th January 1994 submitted by HUDCO, which was conceptually approved by the Delhi Urban Art Commission. Certain clarifications were sought by the Municipal Corporation of Delhi. Municipal Corporation of Delhi approved a revised layout plan for General Pool Housing and Community Center for Sports Authority of India at Pinjrapole, Delhi, approved by the Special Officer exercising the powers of Standing Committee vide decision no. 2508/Standing dated 28th March 1994, subject to the conditions:

HUDCO shall obtain the sanction of the Building Plans from the Building Department of Municipal Corporation of Delhi, in conforming to BBL's/Master Plan 1962. However, the existing structures built up at the site shall be regularized from the Building Department, as per BBL at the time sanction of building plans.

HUDCO shall obtain approval of various services schemes, viz. Water Supply, Sewerage, S.W.D. Roads and Horticulture from respective Services Departments of Municipal Corporation of Delhi, and lay, develop and maintain the same.

HUDCO shall maintain the ROW of Marshal Tito Marg (150 'R/W) and Khelgaon Marg (100' R/W) as per the approved alignment plan, and leave the area affected under road widening if any, free of cost as and when asked for.

HUDCO shall develop the site for 33 KV and 11 KV sub-station, as per approval of Delhi Electricity Supply Undertaking.

The conceptual approval of the layout plan for Andrews Ganj finally was approved by the standing committee of the Municipal Corporation of Delhi vide their Decision No.2508/Sty dated 28th March 1994 as per Master Plan, 1962, wherein the Guesthouses and using a hotel in the

Community Center was not permitted. There were various other conditions stipulated by MCD concerning the approval of drainage and sewerage plans, as well as the sanction of building plans prior to the construction of the buildings.

In view of the offers received from MS Shoes, Phoenix, Asian Consolidated, HUDCO in the 195th board meeting held on 29th March 1994, wherein the members present were Mr. K.K. Bhatnagar–Chairman-cum-Managing Director, HUDCO, Mr. V. Suresh–Director Corporate Planning, HUDCO, Mr. AP Sinha- Director, HUDCO, Mr. RMS Liberhan–Executive Director (Vigilance) (As special invitee), Mr. Gopal Krishan–Company Secretary discussed disposal of properties at HUDCO Place, Andrews Ganj.

HUDCO now has received letters from four private sector organizations showing interest in the purchase of major properties. Copies of the letters are also placed before the board.

M/s Phoenix Overseas Ltd. (2) M/s. MS Shoes East Ltd (3) M/s World Links Hotel Ltd (Part of M/s. MS Shoes East Ltd.) (4) M/s Asian Consolidated Industries Ltd.

M/s. Phoenix Overseas Ltd vide their letter dated 4th April 1994 has indicated to purchase the following Properties:

- 3 acres of Hotel Site plot.
- 9000 sq. meters of land for the shopping complex.
- 2500 sq. meters of land for the Cultural Centre.
- 6 blocks of Guesthouses (B Block)

They have, however, not mentioned the price that they will offer for the above properties. On the contrary, they have asked HUDCO to inform them about the price for the above properties, so that they may negotiate and finalize the deal.

1. M/s M.S. Shoes East Ltd has vide their letters dated 21st March 1994 and 23rd March 1994, and M/s World link Hotels Ltd (sister's concern of M/s M.S. Shoes East Ltd) have offered to purchase the following properties:
    a) Guesthouses—They are willing to buy the remaining nine blocks of Guesthouses. If 9 blocks are not possible, they may be given all 6 blocks of B Block of Guesthouses. They have enclosed a check of Rs 2.10

crores as earnest money of Rs 35 lacs per block.

b) Ground floor of Guesthouses (restaurant/kitchen/shop of the 6 blocks ('B' Block) of Guesthouses. They have enclosed a check of Rs 25 lacs as earnest money.

c) Cultural Land Site- They have offered to purchase the Cultural Land site for Rs 2.00 crores, and they have enclosed a check for Rs. one lakh.

d) Hotel Site–M/s M.S World Links Hotel Ltd (Sister Concern of M/s MS Shoes East Ltd) vide their letter dated 21st March 1994 has offered to purchase the Hotel site Plot at a price of Rs 50 crores. They have enclosed a check of Rs 50 lakhs as earnest money.

We have properties, however, not encased any of the checks sent by M/s. MS Shoes East Ltd/ M/s M.S. World Links Hotel Ltd.

2. M/s Asian Consolidated Industries Ltd vide their letter dated 29th December 1993 has offered to purchase the Hotel site. Cultural site. Guesthouses,

etc as a complete package. However, they have not mentioned any price for the properties, nor have they given any earnest money. M/s Asian consolidated industries Ltd (ACIL) had earlier offered to buy the Hotel site at a price of Rs 53.51 crores when HUDCO had invited a sealed bid in March 1993, but negotiations broke down since they were insisting on combining the Hotel project with other properties. Their earnest money of Rs. 1.00 lakh was forfeited.

a) Since the above four parties are interested in buying the different properties at Andrews Ganj. It is suggested that we may write to these parties (a) M/s Phoenix Overseas ltd. M/s. MS Shoes East Ltd. (C) M/s. World Links Hotel Ltd (sister company of M/s MS Shoes East Ltd) (d) M/s. Asian consolidated Industries asking them to send sealed bids for each property proposed to be purchased by them. No. reserve price will be mentioned. Based on this decision could be taken after considering the offers.

The board, after detailed deliberations, decided that the option for fresh advertisement inviting composite bids for one or more of all properties be resorted to. The board further decided the reserve price for the hotel site should be fixed at Rs. 50 Crores, keeping in view the offers already received and discussions with the Ministry of Urban Development. The reserve price for the shopping arcade and offices should be determined based on the same norms for commercial property as decided in the 181st board meeting.

The board also decided to constitute the Committee to examine and finalize the offers to be received, and also to decide on the incidental terms and conditions, including the reserve price for the shopping arcade. The committee would consist of Chairman & Managing Director. HUDCO- (1) Chairman (2) Joint Secretary (Finance) Ministry of Urban Development - Member (3) Director (Corporate Planning) - Member (4) Director (Finance) HUDCO- Member (5) Managing Director, Tourism Finance Corporation -member.

HUDCO continued to lay hands on the money to be received by selling illegally constructed properties at

Community Center, Andrews Ganj, without any land use and even approval of the layout plan. What to say about building plans? HUDCO's Chairman-cum-Managing Director Mr. K. K. Bhatnagar somehow wanted the 5-Star Hotel Land to go to Asian Hotel Group, and on the other side, the next person in command in HUDCO was Mr. V. Suresh, who was Director Corporate Planning, handling most of the work of Andrews Ganj.

Mr. K.K. Bhatnagar and Mr. V. Suresh never could look into their eyes. Mr. V. Suresh succeeded in not letting Mr. K.K. Bhatnagar succeeded with Asian Hotels, which was obvious - the parallel scene! Dramatis personae: Government of India: General Pool Accommodation for Government Officers: exploiting the Community Center illegally at Andrews Ganj without any land use: unauthorized constructions. All these characters were working hand in hand. They developed a strong bond.

The Indian hotel industry was doing well, and the property prices were increasing like five times, but the land scams were on by the builders and the frauds were growing, and so were the scams in respect of lands and unauthorized constructions were booming. HUDCO along with the ministry in full knowledge was on with concealing the facts of unauthorized constructions because they well knew that justice for the successful allottee is long-drawn and uncertain, due to the long-drawn legal system. They must somehow get the money by selling the properties, as prices of lands had boomed to the maximum, and if they would disclose the truth, then no buyer would come.

Question is, how the Government and HUDCO being a State could conceal such important information at the time of selling the properties to the prospective buyer? Was it fair not to disclose the vital information? Could the hotel operate without the sanction of building plans at the Guesthouses constructed by HUDCO? Could the hotel at Guesthouse blocks be operative without Fire Safety approvals and completion plans of the buildings?

Is it that HUDCO and the Government of India were not notorious for selling the properties without land use and sanction of building plans and the illegal car park construction? Is it not that HUDCO and the Government were hand in glove and were being a genius in constructing 480 rooms with 12 restaurants with no approvals of Municipal Corporation of Delhi, Fire Department, Delhi

Urban Art Commission, Delhi Development Authority, which were one of the mandatory conditions of the allotment of the Andrews Ganj land to HUDCO?

My dear readers, let us dig deeper about HUDCO and Government's genius scam strategy by alluring the investors to give a huge amount of money. The Government and HUDCO had deep digs in the process of constructing the properties with no approvals of the local bodies and besides selling them without disclosing them.

As far as my prudent sense works, the Government and HUDCO together mastered the strategy of grabbing the monies of the corporate in the whole deal to require the investor to go for a ride with nothing in hand. It seems strange that the Government, through the Ministry of Urban Development and HUDCO, handled the whole mechanism of sale of illegal properties. My dear readers, let us elucidate further in the following books coming for further exposure to this scam.

The Government and HUDCO jointly had structured a unique and genius modus operandi of the entire scamming game of illegal properties at Andrews Ganj, and grabbing the monies of the investors.

Let us understand it further, with a clear-cut example and the result, as well as the consequences of the scam. Let us see how HUDCO succeeds in getting the wrongful money by way of unjust riches, by further earning interest in the monies received illegally from the honest investor since HUDCO raised excessive funds by illegal means.

HUDCO and the Government of India (Congress Government) created a maze without letting the prospective investor realize they were just being out-jocked. They were certain Government Officers and HUDCO Officers who had smooth skin in the game, who did not stop scamming the investors towards the Andrews Ganj properties, rather both jointly approved the false informed brochure to allure the innocent investor.

By selling these properties illegally and collecting huge monies for the Government by HUDCO, Mr. V. Suresh, Director Corporate of HUDCO, was a man of excellence, as if he was a magician, for collecting the monies from the Andrews Ganj project.

There is no one in the media in the present scenario with current news to expose the news of the 1989-1994 Andrews Ganj land scam. There is no volcano in the scam brought about by the media of the scam committed by HUDCO, as it is over 24 years and no one has time to spend for such a scam, although the land costing Rs. 5000 crores are wasted since the independence of the country while we are now in 2021.

The needless and willful damage has been caused to the investor depriving of the investments made innocently in the Andrews Ganj land on the deceit of HUDCO and the Government of India, who had a strong bond to get the monies from the unauthorized constructions to let the investor suffer to fill the coffers with HUDCO.
If it was political, then it was different. There could have been a probe against Congress, Government Ministers, Government Officers, HUDCO officers, but no point in a one-man army or private complaint no one pursues, as in the present case of Andrews Ganj land Scam.

Exposed! No, not yet. The progress of this magician, Mr. V. Suresh, would be shown in the later books of this series to come. The unfortunate situation is that the villain of this film was nowhere, as no one was watching the entire story of what to say of the lens. Till now, there has been no one who could rip off the dubious activities of HUDCO and the then Government of India. Even now, such scams do not bother the present Government committed by HUDCO and the then Congress Government.

In the Hudco Land Scam Series, by Alborz Azar reveals the widespread corruption behind the precious Andrews Ganj land in the heart of New Delhi. A media condemned man whose innocence remained unknown struggles with the unfounded accusations which caused public opinion to falter, leading to a guilty sentence before any trial could be scheduled.

The victim behind the scam in this situation was MS Shoes; founder Pavan Sachdeva. Behind the lies and deception, a brilliant entrepreneur took the fall for the underhanded dealings of the Hudco Land Scam.

The same man accused of underhanded dealings fulfilled his debts due to these deceptive lies, with no compensation for the legally awarded settlement. Alborz proves how Pavan's commitment not only caused financial stress on his family, but mental anxiety dealing with this issue for over two decades.

Yet, rulings go unanswered, Hudco ignores legal court findings to repay the ill-gotten monies from MS Shoes. The only response is more excuses as to why the court decisions have not been met by Hudco.

As the culprits hide in the shadows, Pavan struggled through court case after court case, proving his innocence. Official Supreme Court rulings were seen as frivolous orders to corrupt officers and business executives. Alborz brings light on the scam to reveal the truth that has deprived innocent victims of due justice for decades.

alborzaza.net
info@alborzazar.net

HUDCO SCAM SERIES

- **Book One:** Delhi Andrews Ganj Land Scam
- **Book Two:** Government HUDCO Andrews **Ganj Scam**
- **Book Three**: HUDCO Place **Andrews Ganj Land Scam**
- **Book Four:** Andrews Ganj Land Scam Continues
- **Book Five:** Bureaucrats Disputed Bjp Government Ratification of Andrews Ganj Land Scam
- **Book Six:** HUDCO Scammed Leela Hotels as Well - Refunded Entire Amount with Contractual Compounded Interest
- **Book Seven:** HUDCO Place Scam Led Andrews Ganj Project Account to Negative
- **Book Eight:** Courts Concluded HUDCO Scam Defrauded Discriminated Cheated MS Shoes
- **Book Nine:** Government Had No Time to Consider Bureaucrats Ratification of Andrews Ganj Land Scam
- **Book Ten:** Most Awaited Ratification by The Supreme Court of India of Andrews Ganj Land Scam by HUDCO

MS SHOES EAST LIMITED LTD. - PAVAN SACHDEVA STRUGGLING

- **BOOK ONE:** PAVAN SACHDEVA SCAM 1995: K MADHAVAN CBI FORMER JOINT DIRECTOR GAPL SOLICITOR ROLE
- **BOOK TWO:** PAVAN SACHDEVA SCAM 1995: UNDERWRITING PUBLIC ISSUE A FARCE
- **BOOK THREE:** PAVAN SACHDEVA SCAM 1995: A FALSE CASE BY CBI
- **BOOK FOUR:** PAVAN SACHDEVA SCAM 1995: MS SHOES HUDCO GOVERNMENT ANDREWS GANJ LAND
- **BOOK FOUR:** PAVAN SACHDEVA SCAM 1995: 1995 PUBLIC ISSUE AWARDS
- **BOOK FOUR:** PAVAN SACHDEVA SCAM 1995: PAVAN SACHDEVA STRUGGLING

References

Azar, A. (2021, May 3). *IssueWire* . From IssueWire : https://www.issuewire.com/the-hudco-land-scam-series-by-alborz-azar-1698760346491780

HOUSING AND URBAN DEVELOPEMENT CORPORATION LIMITED. (2012, December 12). From https://www.sebi.gov.in/sebi_data/attachdocs/1326777767086.pdf

Housing and Urban Development Corporation Ltd. (n.d.). From https://hudco.org/Site/FormTemplete/frmTemp1PLargeTC1C.aspx?MnId=92&ParentID=305

Ms. Shoes East Ltd vs Housing & Urban Development ... on 3 July, 2010. (2010, July 3). From https://indiankanoon.org/doc/48210005/?__cf_chl_jschl_tk__=522cf46634d97d45f3194ceb9bc4e9c72856496d-1620137702-0-AUVPl1hVMbadgPE6bwolh-dJWuexB2u7J2AgL_Sf97X_z_ajZ1pIC6h5fzoo4DynB6BP1bQkkX9CX4ZtCAZkshScrxNmyfN8ZtjALAk9ZTPee0kUFrFa_g2d5YY9JAtbDybTXCktI_swdl

Municipal Corporation of Delhi. (n.d.). From https://en.wikipedia.org/wiki/Municipal_Corporation_of_Delhi

Made in United States
Orlando, FL
04 November 2026

90206044R00197